DYING AND CREATING

Dying and Creating
A Search for Meaning

by

Rosemary Gordon

London and New York

KARNAC BOOKS

First Published in 1978 by
the Library of Analytical Psychology,
London

This edition reprinted in
2000 with their permission
by H. Karnac (Books) Ltd
58 Gloucester Road
London SW7 4QY
http://www.karnacbooks.com
Copyright © Rosemary Gordon
1978, 2000

British Library Cataloguing in Publication
Data.
A C.I.P. record for this book is available
from the
British Library.

ISBN 1 85575 215 8

THE LIBRARY OF ANALYTICAL PSYCHOLOGY

Edited by

MICHAEL FORDHAM
ROSEMARY GORDON
JUDITH HUBBACK
KENNETH LAMBERT

We shall not cease from exploration
And the end of all our exploring
Will be to arrive where we started
And know the place for the first time.

T. S. Eliot: Little Gidding

Contents

Contents

Editorial introduction

The Library of Analytical Psychology aims to give an account of current developments in that science. In this, the fourth volume of the series, we are adding a new dimension to the topics covered so far. Volume 1 described the evolution of analytic theory, Volume 2 demonstrated some of the changes that have taken place in technique and practice; both contained contributions by a number of writers. The third volume, the first one to be written by a single author, Michael Fordham, made an original contribution to the theory of early development in childhood, to the practice of child analysis and to the study of autism, one of the most obscure areas of childhood disturbance. Fordham's work is based primarily on Jung, though Jung himself had not dealt systematically with either child development or its psychopathology.

The present volume by Rosemary Gordon builds upon, but also transcends, the existing body of theory and practice in another area of analytical psychology. It re-opens one of those topics of universal human concern that so greatly exercised Jung during his lifetime—and indeed Freud also, as well as innumerable other analysts of this century. Gordon brings the themes of death and creativity into meaningful relationship with each other, and in doing so she acknowledges her debt to Jung's creative spirit and his penetrating understanding of death, rebirth and transformation.

This book gives the result of research, devoted to the subject over a number of years, combined with, stimulated by and nourished through the author's analytic work with patients deeply troubled in these areas. The clinical descriptions will assist the reader to share in some degree her experiences and reflections.

As a part of her concern with both normal and pathological reactions to death and creation, she also re-examines those theories of Freud, Klein and Jung that she considers both relevant to her subject and of particular importance in view of recent developments in those schools.

In the field of death, Rosemary Gordon draws, in the first

part of the book, upon a wide area of knowledge, including anthropology, principally in respect of the myths and theories about the origin of death and its symbolic meaning, and of the customs and formal rites that embody attitudes towards the actual dead in various cultures. In addition she also describes the results of Rorschach tests (the standard ink-blot test) carried out by her on four dying patients.

In Part II she examines the development of the symbolic process at length and in a way that, as well as deepening our understanding of creativity, can also help to bridge the split between Freud and Jung over the nature of symbolism.

When dealing with creativity, in the third part of the book, the author analyses the creative process in terms of both its conscious and its deeply unconscious roots, and also draws upon the philosophy and the psychology of art. This is done in a way that can be illuminating to all concerned with art and creativity, including, of course, the psychotherapist, for she describes many of the factors that hinder the creative process and constitute its psychopathology.

Who can die well and create well? Rosemary Gordon gives some answers that are impressively clear and yet open-ended. Certainly they cannot be neglected or denied without the danger of a real diminishment of that ambiguous, ambivalent and bipolar existence that constitutes the human condition.

All the patients discussed in this book completed their analysis several years ago. In any case a great many details of their personal history have been altered in order to safeguard their anonymity.

References to Jung's writings in the volume are taken from the *Collected works*, abbreviated as '*Coll. wks.*', followed by the volume number. Dates refer to the first publication in whatever language and not to the English translation.

The author wishes to express deep gratitude to Corinne Peterson for her work in constructing the index and to James Seddon for his invaluable help with the bibliography. Special warm thanks go to Diana Riviere for her perceptive and speedy editing of this book and the friendship that has grown out of it. The editorial committee is most grateful to both Diana Riviere and John Lucas, who have given invaluable professional help in preparing this volume for publication in addition to its predecessors.

Introduction

One of the most outstanding features in Jung's work is the importance he has attributed to man's drive to create, and to the pervasiveness of man's concern with death. Indeed, one of the factors that first attracted me to Jung's work was the seriousness with which he treated the need to make, that is to create, to invent and to transform; as early as 1929 Jung had classified creativity as one of the five main instincts characteristic of man. As regards death, he believed that there is a natural and innate disposition in man to concern himself with death, and to prepare himself for it as his life moves towards it.

While I responded quickly and easily to Jung's ideas about creativity, my grappling with his thoughts about death and man's concern with it arose from my own analytic experience. For I had discovered, almost to my surprise, that, whatever the age and whatever the symptom picture, sooner or later concern with death becomes a feature in nearly every analysis. Such concern may make its appearance either directly and overtly, or else in a more or less disguised and symbolic form.

It will be the thesis of this book that there is much similarity between the psychological constellation that favours good and peaceful dying and that which favours creative work. In the first part I shall give you my reflections about death as it is experienced in the human psyche. I shall then move on to discuss some thoughts and speculations concerning the creative process. In the final part of the book I shall try to explore the possible parallels and similarities between these two vital human preoccupations and activities.

*   *   *

In this first part, but before I begin to discuss my own thoughts about our concern with death, it might be useful and relevant to start by quoting some of the remarks that Jung himself has made about it, for it is these passages that helped me make sense of my own analytic work and experience.

As early as 1930 and 1931 Jung had written of death as an essential constituent of life. In his paper 'The stages of life' (1930), he remarked:

> As a doctor I am convinced that it is hygienic to discover in death a goal towards which one can strive,

and in 1931 in *The secret of the golden flower*, he wrote:

> Death is psychologically as important as birth and, like it, is an integral part of life.

His most salient points about the psychology of death are, however, to be found in his *Symbols of transformation* (1912) published in 1952. The following is a rather long passage, but it summarises well his general thinking:

> In the morning of life the son tears himself loose from the mother, from the domestic hearth, to rise through battles to his destined heights. Always he imagines his worst enemy in front of him, yet he carries the enemy within himself—a deadly longing for the abyss, a longing to drown in his own source, to be sucked down to the realm of the Mothers. His life is a constant struggle against extinction, a violent yet fleeting deliverance from ever-lurking night. This death is no external enemy, it is his own inner longing for the stillness and profound peace of all-knowing non-existence, for all-seeing sleep in the ocean of coming-to-be and passing away. Even in his highest strivings for harmony and balance, for the profundities of philosophy and the raptures of the artist, he seeks death, immobility, satiety, rest . . .
> If he is to live, he must fight and sacrifice his longing for the past in order to rise to his own heights. And having reached the noonday heights, he must sacrifice his love for his own achievement, for he may not loiter. The sun, too, sacrifices its greatest strength in order to hasten onwards to the fruits of autumn, which are the seeds of rebirth . . .

This passage has strangely close affinities with Melanie Klein's hypothesis that—and I quote from Segal:

> The immature ego of the infant is exposed from birth to the anxiety stirred up by the in-born polarity of instincts—that is the immediate conflict between the life instinct and the death instinct.

As I re-read Jung's passages I was amazed how much my own thinking and experience had in fact run parallel to this

thought, and, indeed, with how much sensitive intuition Jung
has pointed to psychological processes and conflicts that are
the object of much contemporary observation, interpretation,
debate, denial or acknowledgment.

PART I

CHAPTER 1

Social attitudes to death: a brief survey

'Whoever rightly understands and celebrates death at the same time magnifies life.'   *R. M. Rilke*

All my personal experience lends weight to the assumption that death is intimately relevant to all psychological growth. A person's relationship to death, the intensity of his attraction to it, his fear of it, the type of defence built up against conscious awareness of it, the symbolic meaning given to it, all these greatly affect and shape the personality both of an individual and of a culture.

Thus man's greatest achievements, as well as his worst crimes, seem to be, at least in part, an expression of the way he handles his knowledge of the existence of death and it is plausible to believe that only those who can look death squarely in the face can really live a meaningful life.

Several years ago, Arthur Koestler gave voice to this very realisation in a broadcast when he said:

> Take the word 'death' out of your vocabulary and the great works of literature become meaningless; take that awareness away and the cathedrals collapse, the pyramids vanish into the sand, the great organs become silent.

Even a relatively simple people like the Kasai of East Africa were expressing such awareness when they used to say:

> Without magic, illness, knives, arrows, wars and death, life would be just a matter of eating, drinking, sleeping and defecating. Life would be no good without death.

It is, of course, quite true that without death, the death of individuals or even of whole species, there could be no biological change and therefore no evolution of species. Nor is

3

there really any logic in the assumption that man should have been supplied with an innate readiness to live, and with an innate readiness to procreate, and yet be left adrift in his confrontation with that third basic biological process which is to cease to live—that is, to die. Psychological growth, development and the general self-fulfilment of a person seems inconceivable without conscious acknowledgment of the fact of death. In particular the capacity to symbolise—without which all experience is doomed to be without meaning and significance—is likely to remain fallow and undeveloped unless a man live his life consciously aware of death. I hope to give weight to these thoughts in the course of this book.

My interest in this whole problem was aroused first of all not by any personal bereavement, or through contact with people who were actually dying, but as a result of listening to the men and women with whom I sat and to whom I listened in my consulting room. I have tried to listen to them with what I hope is a more or less 'free-floating attention'. Freud has enjoined such free-floating attention on all analysts, believing that they should offer to their patients that same capacity to listen without conscious prejudgment, criticisms and direction that they themselves demand of their patients' 'free association'.

My surprise at this general concern with death is perhaps itself worthy of comment. After all, death is the most certain event in all our lives. It is surely quite unlikely that a person can ever shirk awareness of it for any length of time unless, as I have already hinted, he can relinquish and surrender that gift that marks him as distinctly human: the gift of consciousness of self.

My surprise at the ubiquity in analyses of a concern with death probably reveals how much I had shared in the cultural assumptions and attitudes of my time. For until quite recently modern man had come to regard death as, at best, a regrettable inconvenience, or the result of human inefficiency; at the worst as an obscenity and an outrage. The men of science of our time have had every intention of breaking its pervasive power sooner or later. Thus many of them devote themselves to the task of exploring the possibility of extending life beyond its present span; if possible, indefinitely.

Admittedly, others are engaged in devising ever more efficient means of damaging and destroying life. Such people are perhaps trying to contain their anxiety by putting upon themselves the magic mantle of death, a defensive manœuvre that I shall describe in greater depth when I discuss some aspects of individual psychopathology.

Nevertheless, for at least half a century death has been the most tabooed subject in the Western world—much more so than sex. Geoffrey Gorer, the English anthropologist, has drawn attention to it in an article, 'The pornography of death', which he had published in *Encounter* in 1955. He described there the sense of being isolated and ignored that a person experiences who has suffered the death of a near relative. For the absence of all mourning ritual, and of culturally accepted forms of relationship between the mourner and the rest of the community, had created such general unease and embarrassment that avoidance had become for many the only way out of the dilemma. A particularly interesting study of the psychological literature—or rather the scarcity of the psychological literature—on death was published in 1966 in the journal *Human Relations*, by Mary Williams, an analytical psychologist in London. Having made a thorough survey of 'psychological abstracts' between the years 1931 and 1961, she discovered that the total number of contributions on the theme of death, suicide and murder in 1961 was only a little higher than it had been in 1931, and this in spite of the fact that by 1961 there was a far greater number of workers in the field and a greatly increased volume of psychological literature. This led her to conclude that

> . . . the universal fact of death remained a relatively tabooed subject in Western culture and had, therefore, all the power of a repressed content, seeking a channel of expression.

We may indeed have to examine with greater diligence Kenneth Clark's suggestion that concern with eternity is an important part of every viable civilisation, a suggestion that I have found re-echoed recently in John Dunne's extremely interesting book, *The city of the gods*, in which he writes that:

> It might well be that the stability of Egyptian culture, its persistence for better than two millenia, its ability to recover twice from the kind of downfall that destroyed other civilisations, is not unrelated to the fact that the Egyptian could face death squarely and face it with good hope and had no need to repress the thought of death in order to be happy.

5

From time to time Western man has dared to turn his face from the fact of death in order to contemplate a life without it. The stories of Dr Faustus or of the Wandering Jew spring to mind; and so does Jonathan Swift's *Gulliver's travels*. In one of his travels Gulliver meets the Struldbrugs, the Immortals, and is told that:

> whenever they see a funeral, they lament and repine that others are gone to a harbour of rest to which they themselves never can hope to arrive.

And that 'because of the dreadful prospect of never dying' they are described as

> not only opinionate, peevish, covetous, morose, vain and talkative, but also incapable of friendship and dead to all natural affection.

Indeed, the King of the Luggnaggians teasingly suggests to Gulliver that he should send a couple of Struldbrugs to his own country to arm his people 'against the fear of death'.

In our own time the French writer, Simone de Beauvoir, has in her novel *Tous les hommes sont mortels* once more attempted to explore this theme. The twentieth-century writer can no longer rely on the devil and his pact in order to explain the pain and the hurt of him who cannot die. Rather this pain, this despair, is now recognised as the intrinsic and inevitable component of the fate of a person doomed to live for ever. The hero in de Beauvoir's book is a man who loses, as the centuries pass by, all capacity to see, to taste, to laugh, to cry, to search, to be surprised—all experiences that, as I shall try to show later on, are essential to the process of creation. Instead, everything becomes for him flat, dull, monotonous; and he becomes a 'no-person', neither mean nor generous, neither brave nor cowardly, neither good nor bad. For if time stretches indefinitely then there can be no measure and no meaning. For then there is only:

> always the same past, the same experience, the same reasonable thought, the same boredom. A thousand years, ten thousand years. I can never take leave of myself (p. 229).

And so he is alone. Envious of mortals upon whose lives he tries from time to time to graft his own, he becomes himself envied by those he envies. There can be no pity between him and them; all bonds, all mutuality, all possibility of communication is irrevocably broken once they have discovered

6

his secret. Thus the freedom from death has turned into the curse of an immortality that renders all life vacuous and empty.

I think that Simone de Beauvoir has here described, with great insight, feeling and sophistication, the inner experience of an immortal man. She seems to have little doubt that pain and despair are inevitable components of the fate of a person who cannot die. The world of the immortal man into which Simone de Beauvoir draws us strikes me as remarkably similar to that of the schizoid person who, having attempted to opt out of time, has then lost all sense of time's shape and its human dimension. And so he too is haunted by a sense of isolation, of lostness, of meaninglessness, which then makes him feel like a sleepwalker, like a shadow, stumbling along in a world of men, untouching and untouchable. As Jung has put it in *Symbols of transformation*:

> The neurotic who tries to wriggle out of the necessity of living wins nothing and only burdens himself with a constant foretaste of aging and dying.

I cannot believe that it is only a literary or aesthetic disapproval that accounts for the fact that this particular novel is so little known, for it confirms my own experience that any description of the fearsome and terrifying aspects of immortality tends to meet with surprise, incomprehension and disbelief; as if such awesome possibility is hardly ever contemplated, as if preoccupation with the threat of certain death —sooner or later in our lives—drives from our minds all recognition of the horror of a life without it.

But I had unsought-for confirmation of this fact when a patient, who had been in analysis with me for a long time, and whose horror of and preoccupation with death had haunted her life and cast a deep shadow over it, told me one day that she had just learned of the death of a young colleague—from leukaemia. This news immediately re-evoked apprehension, and hypochondriacal fears re-emerged. Curious, but also somewhat impatient, and disconcerted by the relentlessness of her fear of death, I asked her: 'How would you feel if you knew you could live for ever?' She looked at me—aghast—and just whispered: 'Exhausted'. Then after a while she remarked, almost truculently, 'They ought to play a Requiem not after a person has died, but while he is dying . . . it would make the transition easier ... I thought about this last night when I listened to a Handel concert.' When she discovered that my sympathy and apparent agreement made her truculence unnecessary, she relaxed visibly, and suddenly death seemed to assume a less ominous face for her.

What then, one might ask, has brought about the neglect and the actual avoidance of the theme of death during the first half of this century? Any attempt to answer this question must inevitably remain speculative, but three social phenomena seem to me to have played an important part.

First, there is the rapid and miraculous development of the physical and biological sciences and the consequent expansion of technology. Light without a visible fire; sounds and images heard and seen at a great distance from their source of origin; the control of diseases hitherto regarded as uncheckable and often accepted as the scourges of an inscrutable deity. These and many other thousands of new wonders won by man through his own effort to understand, to control and to bend to his will and to his needs the forces of the universe in which he finds himself—all this has led him to dream that death also can be conquered. And so doctors and the general public, as I have already mentioned, came to share the illusion that death is, after all, merely the result of medical inefficiency, that it can, and should, be avoidable and actually eliminated in the foreseeable future. Suffering, hardship, hurt and loss, it has been assumed, will sooner or later be things of the past. And so science, the offspring of magic, continued to adhere to the objectives and to the ethos of its progenitor; it just carried it several steps further forward.

Secondly, there is the fact of the dramatic reduction of the family unit. The extended family, which included grand-parents, uncles, aunts and cousins, has now shrunk to the small unit of parents and their children. Add to this the increase in social mobility and the housing of people in huge, anony-mous, urban clusters, which deprive the individual of a mean-ingful neighbourhood group, and you get a society made up of people who have very few emotional ties linking them to each other. The rarity of such emotional ties then diminishes a person's possibility of being moved and affected by the loss of any one of them; and he is then unlikely to get involved in mourning rituals. Alienation from the actual experience of

8

losing someone known and cared about is further increased by the fact that dying takes place nowadays in the physically and emotionally sterilised atmosphere of a hospital or a clinic. This makes it even more unreal and not quite imaginable. How much the person in the Western, urban, industrialised world is shielded becomes clear when one talks to or analyses older people, or those from less fragmented societies; many of them seem to have encountered death early in their lives, and often.

The third factor, as I see it, is the decline and the erosion of the religions and traditional faiths, those clusters of beliefs and attitudes that the culture groups used to provide for their members, so that they felt more prepared to act and to react when faced with grief, disaster and death. The modern doctor has rarely been willing to assume a task that has up to now been shouldered by the priest. His science and his preoccupation with his medical techniques have seemed to him to be his natural, indeed his only legitimate response.

During the last few years, however, the theme of death has suddenly re-emerged out of its tabooed position—in the popular press, on radio and television and in scientific writings. What has happened?

The first and outstanding fact is that the honeymoon between man and science is over. One of the turning points appears to have been the development of the H-bomb. Mary Williams, in the survey I have mentioned, did in fact discover what she called 'an explosion of interest in death' in the late 1950s; she attributes this to the 'threat of total annihilation raised by the H-bomb and the atmospheric tests on both sides'. The presence of the H-bomb seems to have forced people to realise that death can indeed once more cover the earth with giant strides, that genocide is a real possibility in our own lifetime, and that science is, after all, a whore who will lie as readily with murder and death as with health and life.

And, although the actual process of dying has been shut away in our hospitals, and although the old—those most likely to encounter death in the very near future—have been banished to 'homes' and 'sunset villages', yet death remains the treasured scoop of the newsman, who is for ever invading our homes, clamouring for our attention, telling his tales of wars, of violence and of accidents all over the front pages of

9

newspapers, and over radio and television. Thus, though the direct and sensuous acquaintance with death has become rare, we continue to be reminded of its existence.

Furthermore—and this is perhaps the most important factor—we can no longer ignore the fact that, in spite of all scientific and technological progress, in spite of increased material welfare and the various benevolent attempts at servicing and social engineering, active death-seeking continues, whether in the form of suicide or murder, whether private or collective. Awareness of this fact is perhaps one of the reasons why an ever-increasing number of people are driven to take a new look at mankind in general and at themselves in particular, to delve more deeply into their inner world and to explore with greater care and diligence the nature and the intensity of the forces at work within them.

These various facts and pressures and this new thrust into the direction of introspection and introversion has paved the way for a re-assessment and a re-valuing of the personal, the experienced, the subjective and the non-material. Perhaps this general tendency also explains why the theories of the Existentialists have become meaningful to a wider public. In their writings, death occupies a central position, precisely because the Existentialist is concerned with man as a conscious being. For the exploration of man as a conscious being who has a deeply-rooted need to establish his own personal identity inevitably leads, I believe, to the recognition that man's attitude to death is vital to the development of consciousness. As Paul Tillich has proposed: 'Being embraces itself and non-being. Being has non-being within itself.' And he illustrates what he means when he remarks that Socrates made it clear that: 'The courage to die is the test of the courage to be.'

The Existentialists attach this great importance to the attitude to death because they believe that it is the relationship to meaning that is for man the most vital question. To quote once more from Tillich:

> Man's being includes his relation to meaning ... the threat to his spiritual being is a threat to his whole being. The most revealing expression of this fact is the desire to throw away one's entire existence rather than stand the despair of emptiness and meaninglessness.

But the search for meaning and for personal identity cannot

bypass the awareness that life is bounded by birth at one end and by death at the other. John Dunne, whose book, *The city of the gods*, I have already mentioned, tries there to provide a comprehensive view of the way in which the various cultures and the various epochs have related to death, either through the myths or through mysticism. The guiding theme in his book is that

> In each society and in every epoch the problem of death takes a characteristic form and receives a characteristic solution.

And he suggests that the existence of death poses for conscious man the question:

> If I must some day die, what can I do to satisfy my desire to live?

He proposes that to begin with there are four main categories of myths through which men try to find a satisfying answer to the question of survival or immortality. He classifies them as follows, taking the myth of Gilgamesh as the most basic and universal one:

1. The myth of the eternal return, usually through rejuvenation, re-assemblage or rebirth.

2. The myth of unending growth, a myth that appears to have been grafted on to the model of the seemingly unending life of trees.

3. The myth of destiny; here death is thought of not as a natural part of all life, but as the outcome of one's destiny.

4. The myth of dualism. This seems to be posed first of all as a dualism between kingship and immortal life, but later on it becomes a dualism between life and knowledge.

Dunne suggests, however, that once man arrives at the concept of a soul, which is thought of as eternal, then the desire for the boundless perpetuation of life loses its force. This leads to the emergence of mysticism; that is, it becomes desirable to escape from the very situation that the myths seek to perpetuate. And then the dualism between life that is good and knowledge that is evil—or at least dangerous to life—is replaced by the notion that it is life that is evil and sorrowful and knowledge that is good, because knowledge emancipates from the evils of life. Dunne then defines mysticism as that conception in which salvation is thought of as a means of liberating man from his 'intemperate will to live' and as having a goal opposed to that of magic, science and religion; for the latter are concerned with the satisfaction of man's wants, while it is the object of the former to do away with them. The two men who most exemplify for Dunne the mystical approach are Socrates and Buddha.

The avoidance of the theme of death during the first half of the twentieth century, as well as its recrudescence in recent years, is in part due to the fact that man can no longer trust and can no longer let himself be guided by collective myths and attitudes about death. This has led him to suspect that he will henceforth have to find and to forge his own personal view, and his own personal relationship to life, to death and to the meaning of it all. In other words the formulating of an attitude and a relationship to death, which up to now the various cultures had assumed to be their task, has now devolved upon the individual.

This search for the meaning of life and the meaning of death is, however, inevitably closely tied up with the search for one's own true self. No wonder that many should at first have shied away from such an awesome venture. For they might well have sensed that it would inevitably involve them in an increased exploration of their own inner world, a deeper knowledge of who and what they are, an expansion of consciousness and confrontation with their illusions, idealisations and shadow side. Ultimately it demands the courage to 'go it alone'. Furthermore, the growing awareness that one's greatest achievements as well as one's worst crimes may be, in part at least, an expression of the way in which one handles the knowledge of one's own mortality must make the task of one's inner search appear all the more urgent and responsible.

Perhaps I should pause at this point. For in any discussion of man's relationship with death, the particular sense in which the actual term 'death' is used must be made explicit; and the particular aspect or the particular context that serves as a focus must be made clear. Many such dialogues founder through lack of clarification on these points. This strikes one when one studies Freud's thoughts about death and the death instinct. Though he states boldly 'the goal of all life is death', yet he also suggests that the death instinct, as opposed to the life instinct, is dumb, a 'silent instinct', whose goal can only be inferred; because, so he argues, there cannot be a concept or a mental representation of death and no direct mental experience of it.

I do not want, at this point, to enter on a discussion of the existence or otherwise of a death instinct; but I am referring here to Freud's remark, because he seems to me to have confused two separate problems: the problem of death as an objective fact and the problem of death as a subjective experience. In other words, one may well want to pose the question —in fact, one cannot stop people from posing the question: what is death really like? What happens when a person—or for that matter any living creature—ceases to be alive? It is a question men have asked ever since they emerged into a state of consciousness. I suspect that this question may well remain for ever unanswered; that none of us will ever know what death is really like; that actual death will probably always remain a mystery.

Even if, however, the actual reality of death should for ever elude us, there is the quite different question that concerns itself with the psychic experience men have of death. For the experience of death seems to me to be a psychic fact, and as psychologists we want to study this experience. Some of us may, therefore, choose to lay aside all questions concerning death as an objective fact, and instead wish to find out what men believe it to be like and to search out man's subjective experience of it. When we do this we then become involved with all the problems associated with man's feelings about death: his fears, his phantasies, thoughts, beliefs, hopes, wishes and expectations. This tends to be my own approach, for I am primarily concerned with death as it is experienced in the human psyche. Many of my formulations are based on my experiences with patients in analysis, who have expressed their attitude to death or their concern with death, or whose symptoms or behaviour patterns have made sense to me only if I recognised them as expressions of, or as defences against, anxiety related to the fact of death.

To cite a few examples:

A young boy, aged seventeen, with many gifts and talents and an I.Q. far in advance of his emotional development, tells me in one session that he has recently been obsessed with the thought of death. He is so terribly aware of the passage of time. He has just realised that he has already lived a quarter of his life. 'I have the odd feeling,' he says, 'that at one moment I am looking forward to something, say a cross-country run, and shortly afterwards I am looking back on it.'

A young woman patient tells me of a nightmare she had while she haemorrhaged dangerously one week after the birth of her child. In this nightmare she sees an endless void that sucks her along; just occasionally there is a point of painful light—this is life—but then she is sucked back and swirled around again in that endless, dark, spiral-shaped void. She was in fact 'sucked' back into this same nightmare every time she fell asleep during the following two to three days, and she became more and more terrified. She had actually been very close to death.

Another patient, a man in his late thirties, had been in treatment for some time. He was successful professionally, but his personal and sexual life had been barren and undeveloped. He had always been pursued by a phantasy that a little boy of about nine years old went to sleep on a window-sill and woke up a wizened little old man with a long white beard. He feared that he would really live out that phantasy. One day he brought the following dream:

> I am on a bicycle; it is a very strange one; I sit very high up on it, as high up as a mountain or a skyscraper. But it is difficult to control the handlebars from there. The wheels are on the ground . . . but they seem far, far away.
> Then I am suddenly on an ordinary bicycle—in an ordinary urban setting. There are people about, but I am almost a skeleton; I can see my flesh disintegrate; it putrefies; it is almost all gone. The bones are not white, as if bleached, but brownish. Actually I am also there as an observer of this skeleton-me. I am terrified that it may terrify the people around me. Then there is also someone else there, a sort of companion; I can't see him, but I know somebody is there. On waking I am amazed that I was not more horrified by the dream, in the dream.

His associations to this dream are really interesting. A day or two before this dream a friend of his older sister had died in St Christopher's Hospital. This is a hospital run by Dr Cecily Saunders specifically for the dying, where they are given quite special care. His sister had several times visited this friend and, in the end, had 'shamed' him into visiting her too. He had been most impressed by the hospital and by the kindness, the aliveness and the gaiety of the staff and of the patients, all of whom knew they were dying.

My patient said that he had felt quite elated after that visit, since he had always been so terrified of death; but he became sad when he heard that the friend had now actually died. He then remembered a friend, an elderly Welsh atheist. One day this friend's mother took to her bed and said she was now going to die. She believed in God; there was no panic. She knew where she was going. So she waited for her death and prepared for it. My patient then told me about himself and that he had no religious beliefs. But he had been much affected the other day when he heard Verdi's 'Requiem'. 'It speaks, it resonates to the non-rational part of myself.'

The over-sized bicycle seemed to symbolise the dreamer's temptation to escape from his earthly bonds. Yet his emphasis that the bicycle's wheels are on the ground shows that there is nevertheless also a wish to remain 'earthed'. In the second part, however, he does become aware that he has a body that is impermanent and liable to decay—but then some sort of individual self can be perceived and he actually acquires a companion.

A gifted young artist, who walked uneasily on the borderline of schizophrenia, brought me a long dream; I will take from it just that part that seems relevant to my theme here:

There is a sea. A sea battle is going on between us and extra-terrestrial beings who have come in flying saucers. But in the end we do get across the water. Then, when we are across it, we are on the final lap to the Gates of Heaven. I tell you—or I think it is my mother—that we must shield our eyes when we get there, as the light would be dazzling and that we have no permission to go inside. My father, who had not come with us, had also been told that we must not go inside. When we get there it is as I had foreseen. And then we are suddenly outside the town where I had been an art student and I point out to you my art college sitting there on the other rock, opposite the castle.

It is when he tells me this last part of the dream that he actually breaks down and cries. After a time he says that he feels like an unfixed photograph which will quickly fade away again. 'And yet,' he continues, 'there are also the two of us, hewn in stone or rock; and we each have a tree that grows and that has arteries and veins.'

These two dreams, dreamed by two quite different people, seem—in the images of heaven and of the over-sized bicycle—to betray the temptation to escape from one's earthly bonds. But both dreamers also try to keep earthed. In the bicycle dream the first patient emphasises that its wheels are on the ground. The second patient in his dream takes the mother/me along with him. In the second part of their dreams both patients become aware of themselves as impermanent and transient, but this perception engenders a feeling of aliveness. In the case of the first patient, the sense of self detaches from the skeleton in the form of the observer and then he actually acquires a companion; the second patient remembers the real thing, his art school—and he actually cries.

The correlation of impermanence with the sense of aliveness in my patients' experience confirms a central theme in my argument: that acceptance of change, the ability to let go and venture into the unknown is an essential ingredient of the art of living. Inevitably, acceptance of change includes acceptance of death, the ultimate and inevitable change. These few examples may be enough to make my point that the theme of death emerges almost inevitably in most analyses.

For the purpose of my studies as an analyst I have, therefore, come to define 'death' as the experience of that particular psychological state, the state of non-being, which might be felt either as a 'dissolution' or as an absorption in a transpersonal union. In either case boundaries are felt as non-existent, and all differentiation, separateness and the tension of opposites seem to have been eliminated. It is, therefore, essentially a non-dualistic state, in which there is no foreground and no background, no subject and no object, no 'I' and no 'you'.

I believe that such an experience of non-being is usual for an infant at the beginning of his life; but I also believe that it remains potentially available to everybody throughout life, through the medium of feelings, of phantasies, images and symbols. In this way it can be almost sensed, almost felt, and certainly wished for. Later experiences, in adult life, may be experienced as re-creations or re-enactments of the original fusion experiences. Thus the nightly withdrawal of consciousness into sleep. Thus the ecstasy of love and passion. Thus the bliss felt, for example, by a dancer who is in complete control of his body and yet feels it to blend with the music, unite with the music, be controlled by the music, in fact, to be an inseparable form of the music. In this union of complete control and complete abandon, a person may feel that he is tasting the very ecstasy of death. Even the revving of a 'plane, which then, through the momentum of its speed, breaks through the bonds of the earth's gravity, may give some people the experience of 'death'—of being all and nothing, no longer a person carried by a 'plane, but himself transmuted into 'plane, speed and space. It would be interesting to know whether something of this kind has been experienced by any of the astronauts.

Having made the distinction between death as objective fact and death as subjective experience, I must now make a second distinction, the distinction between 'death' and 'dying'. Death is a state, a state of which we know nothing except that it is the obverse of aliveness and that it involves the dissolution and corruption of the physical body. When I describe death as the obverse of aliveness I have given what I think is a logically accurate description. But, so far as present-day Western cultures are concerned, the idea of death implies not only that it is opposite to life, but also that it has a definite temporal relationship to it. For we do not think of death as having preceded life, but only as a state that follows life.

Dying, on the other hand, is a process. It is transitory, a movement that changes an organism from a state of being alive to a state of being dead. The exact points at which the process of living ebbs away into the process of dying, and at which the state of death is actually attained, are by no means clearly defined or even universally agreed.

People have been made dramatically aware of this through the recent advances in medicine, and in particular through the organ-transplant operations. Through the excited pronouncements of the mass media, the general public has come to know of problems that had hitherto been regarded as settled; problems such as: when should a person be regarded as legally dead? Should this depend on the cessation of the activity of the heart or of the brain? And how many organs, or even which organs, may a person acquire as substitutes for his own defective ones before he feels himself alienated, a stranger inhabiting a foreign body?

The problems posed by organ transplants; the power of medicine to keep the body alive beyond the point of recognisable psychological functioning, debates on euthanasia—all these open up questions not unfamiliar to anthropologists and students of comparative religion. For the study of different cultures and of different religions has shown that men can think of death in many different ways and even recognise its presence or absence at different points on what one might call the life-death continuum.

For example, in Melanesia death is associated with illness and is thus opposed not—as with us—to aliveness, but to health. In other words, here illness, dying and death are regarded not as qualitatively different, but as part of the process that begins with illness and merely culminates in what we know as death.

In Egypt death was defined in a sense narrower than our own; for there it described only that transition that leads a man from life to the underworld; it was not thought of as death if it led to the world of the gods. Buddhism de-limits the meaning of death to the loss of life of the unenlightened man, of the man who is still chained to the wheel of recurring births and deaths. There is, therefore, no death when enlightenment has been achieved, for then the loss of life becomes the attainment of Nirvana.

In many parts of the world and at many periods in his history man has identified death with birth. '*Mors janua vitae*', said the Romans—'death is the gate of life'; and Mary, Queen of Scots's motto, 'In my end is my beginning', expresses a similar conviction.

This tendency of man to identify death with birth is also reflected in those customs, frequently encountered, in which the dead person is buried in the foetal position, sitting or lying with his knees drawn up. Even today in many societies the identification of death with birth is emphasised by the similarity of the birth and death rituals. Both may involve lustration, bathing and unction with oil and the giving of a special name —to the 'new' body or to the 'new' corpse.

Among the Ashanti of Ghana the equivalence of birth and death rests on the assumption that the 'other world' is a mirror image of 'this world'. The Ashanti express this rather beautifully when they say that:

> Every time an earth mother smiles at the birth of a child, a spirit mother mourns the loss of a child.

One day when walking in the Austrian mountains I found a similar idea expressed with equal beauty and even more economy. I came to a place where a child had been drowned in a brook. The story was engraved in large letters on a stone: '*Das Kind war in den Tod geboren*—the child was born into death'.

Pre-industrial man has in fact often shown remarkable sophistication and psychological insight; this has at times expressed itself in a subtle analysis of the different ways in which a person may die and so reach death. An American anthropologist, J. A. Noon, for instance, has investigated the Ibos of Nigeria from this particular point of view. He discovered that they recognise seven different types of dying, depending on the causes of death, which provoke different emotional reactions and often require different funeral customs. A summary of his findings may here be useful, as it may lay bare some of our more unconscious responses to death.

The best death of all, they say, is the 'death by the gods'. This happens when a man is well advanced in age and has fulfilled his rôle in society; he has completed his life and is able to accept and to prepare for his death.

A second type of death is 'death by misfortune'. In some ways this resembles our own idea of death by accident or misadventure. But while we in the West tend to regard this as due to mere chance—though many of us are now prepared to probe into the possible unconscious motives of the people involved —the Ibos believe that such a death is the work of either witches or evil spirits.

Thirdly, there is 'death resulting from the violation of a taboo'. The Ibos explain this by suggesting that such a violation endangers a person's purity, purity being the natural armour against evil. This explanation also has much in common with our Western thinking about accident-proneness which analysts often discover to be the expression of unconscious guilt feelings and the attempt to relieve these through acts of self-punishment and self-destruction.

Then there is the 'death of a young boy or girl'. Such deaths arouse considerable anger. In such a case the corpse is disposed of by a hurried burial, devoid of the usual rites. Such a death, the Ibos believe, is the result of an oath against this world sworn by the spirit of the boy or girl while it was still in the spirit world; it is a trick they have played on society. Whatever we may think of the cosmological conception behind it, we must, I think, agree that the Ibo seems to have looked squarely and honestly at the psychological reaction to such a death. It is probably true of many people in our own society that the death of a young person, particularly if it seems to be the result of wilful daring, arouses considerable ambivalence and really more anger and resentment than dare be publicly acknowledged.

Another interesting death is the 'death of the repeater child'. If the same parents repeatedly lose a child it is regarded as the same child, which gets itself born and born again only to leave the parents again and again. If the parents' marriage is a bad one, the child, so they think, is unable to stand the bad and quarrelsome atmosphere. But more often the child is regarded as longing to return to its spirit playmates.

A sixth death is the death of a witch whose spell has rebounded.

Finally, there is the death of those who, it is said, have already died long ago. The leper is an example, for his body is thought of as being already in a state of corruption at the time of his actual death. A parallel to this in Western society, with its techniques of prolonging physical life, is the disappearance of personality, of psyche, into a state of senility. When the actual death of such a person occurs the sense of loss is often not very great. He seems to have left—long ago.

The Ibos have conceptualised—and ritualised—the fact that the death of any particular person can arouse in the survivor a multiplicity of complex and conflicting emotions. Among other things they seem to have recognised the fact that one's reactions to the death of another person reflect the emotional ties and relationships one has had with him, as well as one's view of the life he has led and of the death he has died. One may indeed wonder whether the work of mourning is not made easier in a society which so explicitly defines and gives a place to the variety of emotions that we are liable to experience in the presence of a death.

'Experience in the presence of a death . . .' Almost unwittingly, my thoughts have already strayed from a discussion of death as either an objective fact or as a private inner experience to death in the context of personal and social relationships. Indeed, the experience of death has very many facets, which need to be teased apart, for the sake of greater clarity.

For instance, the experience of death usually involves the

reaction to the dead body, the corpse. Fear and terror of the corpse is almost universal in human beings. There seem to be a number of reasons for this reaction; among them, I suspect, is the unease men feel at the stillness and the silence of the corpse. Complete immobility can, indeed, arouse a sense of the uncanny. I suspect, too, that at the back of our minds lurk the belief and fear—or wish?—that the corpse may be just about to move again. Perhaps this explains something of the fascinated horror with which people gaze at snakes and crocodiles in the zoo. But a corpse points to an even sharper ambiguity. For here is an object recognisable as a person; a person who, only a short while ago, moved, breathed, spoke, listened, could communicate, understand and be understood, Now his presence is a deception. Now he is more inanimate than a stone or the trunk of a dead tree. Now he is, as Paul-Louis Landsberg has called it, 'an absent presence, a paradox, baffling and awesome'. And the love that has been felt for the dead person struggles with the horror of the sight of this absent presence and is perhaps further increased by awareness that here is the visible form of death which one day will also leave its mark on the observer.

Again the experience of a death may be determined primarily by the relationship to that other person. If the relationship has been characterised by hatred, envy or rivalry, feelings of triumph or of relief may be provoked. If dependency predominated, panic and despair may be felt excessively. But if the relationship has been one of love and affection then true sadness may be the foremost emotion.

Thus all feelings in the presence of death are likely to be strong and complex. As Landsberg has said in his sensitive essay, 'The experience of death':

> We constitute a 'we' with the dying man and thus are led to an experiential knowledge of our own mortality.

Indeed, in spite of the vast amount of energy deployed by some in their attempt to construct barriers against awareness of their own mortality, the fact of death is really too insistent, too pervasive, for such manœuvres to be effective. A man may kill a thousand others, yet even this will not protect him from the knowledge that every one of his victims is really but a token of his own vulnerability, of his own inevitable end.

The fact that the awareness of our own mortality can render —and does in fact render—our lives more valuable, more precious and more worthwhile, is something that technological man had almost forgotten. Only a few poets, artists and philosophers have kept alive for us the knowledge that death is in fact indispensable in order to give life both zest and meaning.

The study of death as experienced in dreams, imagery and symbolic forms, in art, poetry and music, reveals that man carries inside him a whole iconography of death. And, in the course of observing, both in myself and in my patients, thoughts, phantasies and feelings towards death, I have come to the conclusion that death has a thousand faces. It may show itself as friend or foe, isolating or uniting, eerie or cosy, raping or loving, the axe or the cradle, light or dark, barren, rank and putrid, or rich and fulfilling. Each one of us sees only one of these faces at a time, and perhaps only a few in the course of our whole lives. These thousand faces of death shift and weave complex patterns, which harmonise and express our different moods and our different preoccupations at any particular time; and they reflect the personal past from which we emerge and the different goals we choose to pursue.

Death then, I suggest, is used by the psyche as a symbol for experiences of fusion and union, and of the experiences of the dissolution and surrender of conscious, personal existence. And men are capable of experiencing not only aversion but also attraction towards death. I will argue this further later on. The existence and perhaps the danger of this attraction is rarely admitted by Western man—yet it is recognised in Buddhism where the 'death-wish' is named and is actually condemned as the third of the three 'cravings', the other two being the craving for sense-pleasure and the craving for becoming. His attitude to death and the relationship to it that has evolved affects a man's whole psychological development and growth. Thus an excessive fear of death—being often a defence against an excessive desire for it—can inhibit the development of consciousness and the capacity to grow and to tolerate change. For example, the patient who had the bicycle dream, and who feared that he would 'sleep away his life', was clearly, in a large part of himself, longing to die, as a means of rejoining his mother. He had lost her 'psychologically' when he was evacuated at the beginning of the war; and he had lost her 'really' when she died of hyperthyroidism before his final return to London. As a matter of fact he had impetuously and impulsively come to London in the middle of a term—he knew not quite why—but he arrived just as his mother was collected by the ambulance and taken to hospital—where she died a few hours later. His memory of her, and of his childhood with her, emerged only slowly and painfully as if out of a big black hole of oblivion. And though I rarely felt myself to be out of touch with him, he frequently felt that he had hidden himself from me, that he had kept himself 'on the other side of a stream'. One day he had a dream in which he heard his mother say quite distinctly: 'You have not come to see me since you were very small.' But her remark, he explained, was not reproachful but warm and loving: and the dark in which he found himself with her was not frightening, but strangely pleasant.

Relationship to death also affects, I believe, a person's capacity to enjoy repose, silence and sleep. One patient who had been haunted by the fear and terror of death suffered much from insomnia: she feared that if she slept she would miss something. Another patient's rebellion against personal mortality had led him to develop a complicated theory about the biological possibility of constant physical growth and renewal, a theory in which death was considered an unnecessary accident, or else as somebody's wilful withholding from him of the right ingredients necessary for his well-being. He was, in fact, an incessant talker, who found silence awesome and quite intolerable. He died, a few years later, relatively young, of cancer—that illness in which growth gets out of hand, goes mad and destroys the organism itself. Relationship to death affects also the capacity to experience excitement and ecstasy —and yet, without the capacity to really surrender to love and to the forces of one's own receptive or creative imagination, life will inevitably remain flat, dull and meaningless.

The sort of defences that can be developed against any awareness of one's mortality could thus be summarised as follows:

1. One may try and forget its existence altogether.
2. One can try and remain hyper-busy and hyperactive; but then one might end up by not even being able to sleep.
3. One may deny one's own mortality by deluding oneself

that death is just an accident, an inefficiency, something that man will one day manage to eliminate.

4. One can try and identify with death. This seems to be one of the roots of sadism. The sadist seems to be the person who identifies with the invulnerable destroyer; and he projects the unconscious acknowledgment of his own mortality on to his victim.

5. One can try to 'stay put' and so stop growth and development. As Jung has put it:

> The neurotic who cannot leave his mother has good reason for not doing so. Ultimately it is the fear of death that holds him there.

This leads me now to return to my opening remarks and to reflect that man's ability to symbolise, which is surely one of his most important and one of his most essentially human functions, is deeply dependent on his capacity to expose himself to the experience of death. I will spell this out in greater detail in Part II. But suffice it here to say that the ability to symbolise, which is the most essential ingredient in all creative endeavour, rests very firmly indeed on the capacity to accept both activity and passivity, the forces of life and the forces of death, tensions and effort as well as surrender; in short, it involves the coming to terms with paradox.

I want to end this first chapter by describing a personal and very interesting experience that confirmed some of my reflections about the rôle in life of the awareness of death. I had the opportunity to participate in a workshop on group analysis. The workshop lasted one week; all participants were group analysts and many of them were also trained psychoanalysts or trained analytical psychologists. We met every day in small groups of eight, in seminars, in structured lecture and discussion groups and also in a large unstructured group.

The experiences in the large unstructured group were particularly intense, often anguished and painful, but also exceptionally exciting and thought-provoking. Many members admitted that they felt almost psychotic anxieties; there was a feeling about of 'eat or be eaten'. There was a fear that one might be pushed back to the very edge of one's own identity; and several members spoke of it as a life and death struggle.

After a time we came to recognise that this life and death struggle was intimately related to the fear of losing oneself; to the fear that one might be sucked into an anonymous crowd, into a collectivity; that one might forget one's own identity, or that one might be stripped of it; or that one might just not be recognised.

The experience in the large group contrasted strongly with the experience in the small groups, where personal and inter-family themes and conflicts tended to predominate and find expression. But in the large group there emerged quite spon-taneously grand mythological, that is archetypal, themes; themes of witches, goddesses and guardians of the threshold. These themes seemed to constellate the life and death ex-perience of our identity crisis; they seemed to express the in-tensity of this crisis and at the same time, by giving it a form, they became themselves a mode of its transformation.

I was impressed that the theme of death should so readily emerge and impose itself, and that so many members should be led to recognise it—after a time—as a valid symbol to express surrender to a state of confusion which, if accepted, could become potentially a state of creative confusion.

This personal experience thus confirmed for me once more, in a very direct and emotionally impressive way, that the moment of blankness and extinction can become, if recognised and accepted, the moment of incipient fruitfulness, and that ac-ceptance of death is truly the final test of the acceptance of reality.

CHAPTER 2

Freud, Jung and the death wish

Inevitably, a concern with the theme of death forces one to re-examine the theories developed about it by Freud and Jung.

Only the greatest minds seem able to burst through their cultural constraints, only they seem willing and able to explore tabooed subjects and to see where the majority is handicapped by blind spots. Both Freud and Jung took up what had been so neatly swept under the late nineteenth and early twentieth century carpets—the subject of death. And, as I have already pointed out, both turned their attention to this fact in man's life, and concerned themselves with both his conscious and his unconscious feelings and reactions to it. And both believed that the knowledge of his own impermanence and mortality acts in man as a major force in his psychic life and development.

But they were ahead of their time, and their adherents did not find it easy to follow them so far. The disciples of Jung tended to relegate concern with death safely to the second half of life, while Freud allowed his concept to be hedged around with all sorts of limitations.

When Freud first proposed the existence of a death instinct or Thanatos in 1920, he argued that every fundamental physiological process must have a mental equivalent, an instinct. And so he postulated the existence of a death instinct as the psychic equivalent of those physiological processes that lead to a reduction of differentiation and to the reinstatement of an earlier state; as examples of such physiological processes he mentioned the process of katabolism and the constant dying and re-creation of cells. This is how he expressed his thoughts in 1920 in 'Beyond the pleasure principle':

> ... the ruling tendency of psychic life, perhaps of nerve life altogether, is the struggle for reduction or removal of the inner stimulus tension—the Nirvana Principle, as Barbara Low puts it—a struggle which comes to

expression in the Pleasure Principle and is indeed one of the strongest motives for believing in the existence of the death instinct.

At that time Freud thought of the death instinct as the origin of the 'wish' and of the 'need' to return to an earlier state of existence; and that this expresses itself in what Romain Roland had suggested might be called states of 'oceanic experience'.

Most psychoanalysts, however, including Freud in his later years, could not accept that the death instinct might possibly express itself directly in terms of an actual wish for death or even in the capacity to have a mental representation of it. Instead they came to believe that the death instinct is really a 'silent' or a 'dumb' instinct, and that it can therefore express itself only in terms of either a fear of death or as aggression. And they thought of the forces of the death instinct as forces that were only directed outwards, that is away from oneself.

In a very scholarly discussion of the concept of the death instinct, published in 1953, Flügel cited the various phenomena that he thought had contributed to the formulation of the death instinct. As a first point he cited there the 'universal tendency of organisms to die', and commented that:

> this most fundamental and obvious implication has received little direct treatment in psychoanalytic literature, and contributions have been made under headings other than the straightforward need to die.

In fact, as was shown by Brun in 1953, few psychoanalysts have been able to accept at all the death instinct hypothesis. And yet without it Freud's fundamental concept—that the dynamics of psychic life are based on the energy evolved, or released, in the struggle between opposing forces—is seriously weakened, as Norman Brown among others has convincingly argued.

Admittedly the concept of the death instinct has assumed a central position in Melanie Klein's theories. But here too the expression of the death instinct is only thought of in terms of the experience of a *fear* of death.

> 'I suggest', she writes in *Theory of anxiety and guilt*, 'that the primary danger situation arising from the activity of the death instinct within is felt by him (the infant) as an overwhelming attack, as persecution.'

Thus Melanie Klein agrees with the later Freud that Thanatos cannot be experienced directly, that is as a wish or a longing for death; but that it can only be felt, and that its presence can only be suspected, because of the presence of emotional reactions against its promptings. It is thus the presence of very early feelings of hate and destructiveness that, according to Klein, lead us to suspect that there must exist a death instinct.

There is no concept of a death instinct in Jung's metapsychological schema, and he has often been criticised for his monistic view of libido. I suspect, however, that the difference between Freud and Jung concerning the concept of libido may be the result of the use of different levels of abstraction. Discussing Freud's death instinct theory, Jung wrote in his *Two essays on analytical psychology* that

> ... what Freud probably means is the essential fact that every process is a phenomenon of energy, and that all energy can only proceed from the tension of opposites ... it is sufficiently obvious that life, like any process, has a beginning and an end, and that every beginning is also the beginning of the end.

In the same paper Jung writes a footnote in which he claims that 'This idea [the death instinct] came originally from my pupil Dr S. Spielrein, of "Die Destruction als Ursache des Werdens", Jahrbuch für p.a. psychoanalytische und psychopathologische Forschungen, IV (1912, 465ff). This work is mentioned by Freud who introduces the destructive instinct in his "Beyond the pleasure principle"' (Two Essays, p. 27). And in his essay on 'Psychic energy', Jung defines 'libido' as a 'hypothetical life energy resulting from the tension of the opposing life and death forces'.

Like Freud, Jung saw death in terms of the homeostatic process. 'Life is an energy process,' he writes, 'and like every energy process, it is in principle irreversible and is therefore directed towards a goal. That goal is a state of rest.' But, unlike Freud, Jung believed that the psyche of man concerns itself directly, spontaneously and naturally with death and with the process of dying. For just as 'nature prepares itself for death, so does man'. And, so he argued, just as the thoughts of a *young* person, when he has time and leisure for daydreaming, tend to be concerned with anticipations and are, as it were, preparatory acts or even psychic exercises for dealing with future realities, so, if we did investigate the ageing person, we should probably also find a surprisingly large number of anticipations, including death; for 'willy-nilly, the ageing person prepares himself for death'. And he remarks, challengingly, that 'it is just as neurotic in old age not to focus upon the goal of death, as it is in youth to repress phantasies which have to do with the future'.

Jung was in fact very interested in man's relationship to death and in the symbols that the psyche evolves around this theme. In many ways his conception of man's attitude to death resembles that of the Existentialists. Tillich, the Existentialist theologian, for instance, postulated three basic existential anxieties—of death, of meaninglessness and of condemnation. All these, he suggested, really represent the basic fear of non-being. Neurosis, Tillich argued further, is a way of avoiding non-being by avoiding being, for unless man faces up to and deals with the fear of his inevitable death, he cannot develop the capacity to live. Jung really makes the same point when he writes that, '. . . the neurotic who cannot leave his mother has good reason for not doing so; ultimately it is the fear of death that holds him there'. And in another essay he writes: 'The refusal to live is the same as the refusal to die', and he claims to have observed that the person who shows fear in the face of life often shows it later in the face of death.

Before I describe some case material, to illustrate the value of the concept of a death wish and what use I have made of it, and before I discuss in the next chapter a pilot study designed to test Jung's thesis that the psyche of man tends unconsciously to prepare for death, I must summarise how I think of the various stages and phases of psychological development that are relevant to the themes of death and of creation.

I believe it is implicit in Jung's theories that psychological development, like physical development, proceeds *not* from chaos to order but from a state of relatively undifferentiated unity, through the process of differentiation, towards states of ever more differentiated unity. To map out very briefly the major phases:

There is an original experience of mother–child unity. This is particularly strong while the baby is still *in utero*. It is experienced probably not only by the baby but also by the mother.

But it is important not to blur the difference between an actual 'fact' and a description of 'experience', for this often creates unnecessary misunderstanding and controversy. It is a *fact* that mother and child and even mother and foetus are not identical, but it is also probably a fact that the unborn organism experiences its own separateness very much less before birth than after birth. There are a good many reasons for such a hypothesis:

(a) The conditions of the foetus do not really favour the experience of boundaries, of separateness or identity. He lies in water, which must damp down the physical experience of a boundary; he feeds through the placenta and so can have little sensuous experience of hunger or cold or thirst.

(b) Experiments with people placed in a stimulus-free environment—that is, conditions approximating to the intra-uterine state—have shown that even grown-up and mature people can lose their sense of identity, some sooner, some later and become confused or even hallucinated.

Birth is a violent and radical change of state. The individual is thrust out and exposed to an onrush of sensuous stimuli—light, sound, temperature, hunger, etc., etc.

It seems as if at first both mother and infant try to re-create the pre-natal state, as nearly as possible: the baby sleeps and so withdraws from the world as much and for as long as possible. He is intolerant of strong stimuli.

The mother, from her side, seems anxious to keep the baby as close to her body as possible, and to respond quickly to all his needs—in fact, if possible, to anticipate them.

Thus the behaviour and the reaction of both mother and baby seem designed to prolong the experience of fusion beyond the time of the actual birth. And thus are delayed, for a while, such experiences as 'I' and 'not-I', of 'inside the body' and 'outside the body'.

It does seem to be the case that the baby's experience during the first few days after his birth tends to polarise into 'good' states of relaxation and 'bad' states of tension, due to need from within and impingement from without. In other words, pleasure, at this stage, lies in states that approximate as closely as possible to the pre-natal state: no stimuli; no wants; no tensions; no sensations; no boundaries.

This then seems to approximate to the state that Freud has described as 'oceanic'; and which may be the prototype of the state of 'bliss', a state men tend to seek throughout their lives.

Jung gave us the concept of the 'self' to describe that part of the psyche that is concerned with the experience of wholeness and with the production of images and symbols of wholeness. The self can also be thought of as the source of those mental drives and forces that seek and strive for wholeness.

Fordham's term 'the original self' suggests that this first state is an early and primitive form of what later becomes a complex and sophisticated goal. He thus produced a firm theoretical foundation for the belief that development proceeds from simple order to an ever-increasingly complex order.

Clearly these 'self' experiences can no longer be easily denied or overlooked. Their presence seems also to have intrigued and challenged many psychoanalysts. This has then provoked them to evolve some conceptual framework within which it can be named, described, accounted for and understood. And so we find in the psychoanalytic literature terms like

> the primitive ego (Fenichel)
> or
> the ego-cosmic phase (Federn)
> or
> the primal psychophysical self (Jacobsen)
> or
> the true self (Winnicott)
> or
> the level of Creation (Balint).

I suspect the difference is primarily a verbal one. The names chosen point, however, to a difference of emphasis on either structure or experience.

But to continue my description of the developmental schema: maturation—plus the existence of the external world and of the character of the people around him—soon reduces the frequency and the intensity of the baby's idyllic state of fusion, of 'non-being'. His own needs begin to emerge, to be experienced, to differentiate and to clamour for attention. They drive him towards active seeking, active avoiding and towards the dawning recognition of himself as a separate entity in the world. The forces that determine what needs, what impulses and what phantasies the infant will come to experience, and to which objects in his world he will direct his interest and his readiness to perceive, to attend and to act—these forces have been variously described as 'instincts' or drives, as innate release mechanisms by the ethologists or as deintegrates by Michael Fordham.

The interdependence of drive and mental representation or of predisposition and experience is made explicit in Jung's theory of the archetypes. In his commentary on *The Tibetan book of the dead* he writes that:

> Inherited archetypes are devoid of content because, to begin with, they contain no personal experiences. They only emerge into consciousness when personal experiences have rendered them visible.

Jung thought of archetypes as psychosomatic entities—having a *physical* expression in the form of instinctive activity and a *mental* expression in the form of images. Archetypal images, he claimed, represent the goals of the instincts, which they thus transform into psychic and therefore into potentially conscious experience. The concept of the 'unconscious phantasy', which Melanie Klein developed, and which she defined as the 'mental expression of instinct', is strangely analogous to Jung's concept of the archetype.

The relationship of the model of the instincts and the model of the archetypes as the basic motivators and organisers of human behaviour and development might best be considered in terms of Heisenberg's principle of Uncertainty. Heisenberg had advanced this principle in order to account for the fact that physicists can understand light both in terms of waves and in terms of particles. In analogy we can look at behaviour either in terms of instincts, drives, deintegrates, resistances and defences—that is, in terms of the energic *processes*—and this could be compared to the wave theory of light; while the understanding of behaviour in terms of the patterns and interactions of the mental *contents*—both archetypal and acquired—would be parallel to the particle theory of light.

The infant's increasing awareness of *himself*, of his needs and of the world around him, leads gradually to a recession of his need for fusion. It seems to me that it is during this period that the life and the death forces differentiate from each other—fusion remaining the goal of the death wish and de-fusion, separateness and identity, the goal of the life wish. And because, according to Jung, 'instinct' has its own characteristic mental representations, the life wish and the death wish tend to be accompanied by and to express themselves in archetypal images.

As a result of the differentiation of the life force and the death force, the two major psychic systems, the ego and the self, come to be experienced as if they were separate; indeed, at times they may be experienced as if they were mutually exclusive and opposed to each other. Thus each of them, the ego and the self, comes to symbolise the two goals of the two major instincts: the drive towards separateness, uniqueness, identity and achievement—with all the images associated with one's own body and one's own personality—is then felt as the symbolic manifestation of the ego; while the need for fusion and wholeness—with the associated phantasies of a re-entry into the mother's breast or belly, or a re-fusing with Mother, Nature or Universe—is felt as issuing from the non-ego, the self.

The concept of the self really serves a dual function. When used in a structural or metapsychological model it refers to the wholeness of the psyche, and includes the conscious as well as the unconscious, archetypal and personal experiences, and ego and non-ego functions. The existence of all these different systems is the result of the 'spontaneous property of the self to deintegrate', Fordham having defined the self as a 'dynamic system that deintegrates and integrates in a rhythmic sequence' (Fordham, 1969).

But the concept of the self, as a system distinct from the ego, does service also in an experiential model; for we need to make sense of our subjective experience. Thus the self has been invoked as the source and the object of the many symbolic representations of wholeness, such as the mandala, the philosopher's stone, the child, the tree, etc. Since we believe that drives and phantasies are closely intertwined, the existence of such phantasies and symbols of wholeness must lead us to postulate the existence of a distinctive drive towards wholeness, be this accomplished through fusion, through projective identification or through ordering, synthesising, regression or progression. Thus, when we deal with actual experience we cannot but recognise that the ego and the self are often felt to be the repositories and the guardians of our two major instinctual goals: the ego being primarily concerned with separateness, the self with wholeness.

As the infant's powers of awareness and discrimination develop, so he becomes ready to de-fuse or to differentiate psyche from soma. This is a very important phase; for with this differentiation of psyche from soma he slowly develops a sense of *psychic* reality. That is to say, he begins to sense that he has an inner world of his own, filled with wishes, hopes, images and phantasies. And he learns that he can control them, manipulate and 'play' with them. When this sense of an inner world of one's very own has started to consolidate, then the infant becomes progressively more able to bear some frustrations and discomforts. For he can now carry inside him images of the desired objects and persons, such as the mother; and he can evoke in himself these images at moments when the actual person or object is absent and unavailable. If the absence is not excessively long, then he can hold on to these images, and so span the frustrating gap between need and satisfaction. The success with which he does this helps to assure him of the existence of this inner world; assures him that he can keep safe his images and memories in this inner world, that this world belongs to him alone, and that because of it he has indeed a certain amount of independence and autonomy. The achievement of such trust in his own inner world is vital for individual development and for the capacity to create—to invent, to discover, to play and to explore—for ultimately such activities rely on the deep-seated faith that one is not hollow, or empty or helpless.

I think that it is precisely Jung's conception of a self and of an ego that helps us to recognise and to understand man's bivalent feelings about death; it helps us to perceive that there must be a permanent state of tension between the demand for separateness and the demand for union; between the drive towards differentiation, and the drive towards non-differentiation. Thus the experience of death, of non-being, and of the various symbols of death are, I suggest, felt to be under the aegis of the self, while a conscious awareness of death and of dying is a psychological experience that can exist only when an ego-structure has already emerged. It is only when I experience myself as 'I', when I feel a sense of identity, of existing, that I can be said to have an ego. Dying then is the experience of a loss of this ego. Freud also seems to have been aware of this and Jung recognised it when he remarked that:

> When Freud coined the phrase that the ego was the true seat of anxiety, he was giving voice to a very true and profound intuition. Fear of self-sacrifice lurks deep in every ego.

Different parts of the body and even of the mind may be lost without its being felt as a dying. But the threat of *ego* disintegration, as experienced, for instance, by the incipient schizophrenic, is often felt as an impending death, and as a threat of total annihilation. Patients on the brink of psychosis may express what they feel either directly as a fear of death, or they may portray it in such images as 'being sucked into a dark tunnel' or as 'being thrown by a wave into the mouth of a whale'—images which, by the way, clearly identify death with a re-fusion with the Great Mother, and with a return to the womb, the cosmic womb. In other words attitudes to death and to dying, including the fear of death and of dying—which, by the way, declines in senile dementia—can be experienced only when an *ego*-structure has emerged, that is, when an individual has discovered and acknowledged his separateness and so has assumed the tasks of being 'conscious'.

Consequently the death instinct, or Thanatos, which Freud proposed in order to account for the tendency of organisms to revert to a less differentiated state, might be translated into Jungian terms and described as the valence of the self, that is as the attractive force of the self. This attitude to death depends on the interaction and interdependence of ego and self and on the kind of equilibrium established between them and the relative 'trust' achieved between them.

The following case histories may make clear what I mean:

The first patient I want to describe is Clare, who started analysis when she was about twenty years old. She spoke in a soft, timid voice. For a long time she never looked at me and for a long time she sat on the edge of her chair, never taking off her coat. The use of the couch seemed out of the question. She wore loose coats and a scarf around her neck in both winter and summer.

She was afraid of travelling in buses and subways. She was afraid of crowds. She was exceedingly noise-sensitive. She had been anorexic during adolescence and had been hospitalised for eighteen months. She still had some eating difficulties, which now took the form of various food fads. She often expressed suicidal ideas and wishes.

Early in her analysis her hostile feelings towards both her parents emerged. They had in fact separated when she was twelve years old. She feared that both of them would want to suck her dry of any good things that she might possess. If she got better as a result of analysis then she would have to pass on the benefits to them. Whenever she met her mother, or if she discussed her in a session, this created painful states of panic and despair. It was then that she felt most strongly and expressed most strongly her wish to die or to go mad. 'I wish I could go mad; then I could die and not feel guilty.' At such moments she felt she had turned to stone. The wish to go mad was sometimes expressed directly, and sometimes it was projected on to the parents; they were then thought of as wishing her to be mad—or dead.

The fragility of her ego structure was shown in the way she felt 'ground down' in a crowd. 'It feels like being on a conveyor belt, relentless, grinding.' And one day she described the conveyor belt as 'black and white, broad and thin, light and dark, and it has a sound to match the broad-thin. It is a screeching deadness.' In this image then the opposites were fused. She also feared she would be swamped by her family and sucked down into them. One day she remarked: 'I am not a Me. I am only a something.' And she then described states of dissociation that she had experienced as a child:

> It felt like a fourth dimension. Like stepping into space; like being the universe. It is like looking at one's hand under water and because there is the water, the hand does not seem to belong to me.

The wish to become a cabbage or to go mad or to die recurred for a long time at moments of conflict or crisis. Improvement or an increase in awareness and consciousness was often felt by her as too painful, too great a price to have to pay.

> It is too much for me; I have not got it in me. I don't passionately want to be dead but I see no reason to be alive. There is too much pain in it. I can't take any more.

But one day after a nightmare, which took her back to her war experiences during the bombing of London, she actually began to experience and to express a fear of dying.

Yet it was probably the very forcefulness of her death wish that had kept the war experiences as a living reality inside her; it was a long time before she could hear the sound of aeroplanes without feeling an uncontrollable panic.

The forcefulness of the death wish was shown in the precariousness of her ego-boundaries: in her readiness to experience confusion and panic; in the defensive barriers she had to erect against invasion from outside; in her avoidance of looking and being looked at; in her experience of being swamped and ground down. And, because of the pull-back towards the original self she could only maintain what ego she had with the help of a great deal of scaffolding: she could not, for instance, allow herself to experience any good or affectionate feelings for anybody. She was quite willing to admit to feeling anger and rage and hatred; but the possibility of feeling love terrified her. In her relationship to me she behaved like a timid forest creature, whom one must feed without either side acknowledging that this is happening. Transference interpretations did not seem to be heard, though later on she would say something that made it clear that she had in fact internalised them—surreptitiously, as it were. And death, the submergence of consciousness, and the loss, or the surrender, of identity were constantly and ambivalently experienced themes.

It is probably quite clear from my description of Clare that I learned an enormous amount from her and that I owe her a great deal. I have often thought that Jung was able to recognise the existence of the death wish, while Freud could not really do this, because Jung, unlike Freud, worked with psychotic patients, that is with those patients who are so patently an arena of the full and untamed forces of life and death.

The second patient I want to describe is Patrick, a broad, tall and highly intelligent man, who was thirty-seven when he started analysis. His mother had been an upper-class woman, not married to his father, but who had three children by him. Socially she passed them all off as her adopted children and so earned herself the reputation of being a generous and socially conscious person.

The patient had slept in his mother's bed until a very late age. He never could remember at what age he was 'thrown out'. But he remembered experiencing all sorts of anxieties and phantasies in this close contact with his mysterious mother. And he remembered that at times he would put on all available clothes before going to bed at night—as if he needed many thick layers of protective clothing.

Early in his analysis he had a dream in which his mother chided him because he had crept out of a bed that she had ordered him to share with a lion.

It is hardly surprising that in his analysis Patrick often

experienced very strongly hostile and paranoid feelings towards me. Over a long time he tried to manipulate the transference situation into a sado-masochistic love-battle. He experienced me as cold, as predatory. He described me as a fish hiding under a stone, shooting out a long tongue to catch its victims. But I was also felt as withholding from him my secrets, my powers, my knowledge and my love. I set traps for him, so as to confuse him. At other times he would try to entice me, or to command me to chase him with questions, to press his secrets out of him, to argue with him, to fight with him.

Although he expressed considerable hostility, anger and aggression, yet he thought of himself as soft, as flabby and squashy.

Unlike Clare, who longed for death though she also feared it, Patrick looked upon death as his arch-enemy with whom he must engage in battle. In his love affairs he acted out his identification with an over-possessive, devouring but all-providing Artemis mother; when he masturbated he usually had masochistic phantasies in which he sacrificed himself to the Artemis-mother.

He told me that the victim of Artemis must always be a beautiful, perfect and intelligent youth who is beaten to death.

Whenever the theme of death came up in the sessions Patrick experienced great tension, anxiety and anger. At the end of one such session he shouted at me with a mixture of rage and despair: 'What is the good of it all? You can't cure me of the ultimate disease: Death', and he did not come back to analysis for three whole weeks. The first remark he made when he returned was: 'I have only come back to spite my mother's ghost.' This made it very clear that he experienced analysis as a way of rescuing himself from the death-giving forces within himself.

In the case of this patient, the ego-functions seemed to have jelled sufficiently so that he could experience some sort of structured battlefield inside him. He was not, unlike Clare, consciously drawn towards death, towards the experience of merging and dissolving and unconsciousness. Rather he tried to defend himself against what he felt as the overpowering threat of the death forces within him by becoming death, by identifying with death, which had come to be personified for him in the form of the death-wielding mother-goddess. But he revealed, in the phantasy of the perfection one must attain in order to 'deserve' death, that there was also a strong, even if only unconsciously experienced, attraction to death inside him. He was indeed caught in the sort of double-bind which I have observed in many other patients. If you are really good and loved, then you must die; if you are alive then it means that you are not good, not perfect, not really loved. It is a theme that I have observed in particular patients whose older siblings had died in early childhood and had subsequently been idealised by the parents.

My third patient is Fred, a manic-depressive man who came into analysis because of his fear that he might again develop a duodenal ulcer. He was a warm, sociable, outspoken and talkative business man. His affects flowed freely and it was easy to recognise and to respond to them. He was married, had children, had many friends and was involved in many social activities. He seemed firmly rooted in the social matrix from which he came, the non-conformist lower middle class.

Fred had experienced with great pain the death of his brother-in-law, who had died of a perforated ulcer. He had loved and hero-worshipped this brother-in-law ever since his early teens.

It was thus a true—and relatively realistic—fear of death that had brought this patient to analysis. He hoped that analysis would prevent the recurrence of his duodenal ulcer.

Only after six months of analysis could Fred broach the subject of death—apart from having mentioned it in his initial interview. When he did start to speak of it he admitted that he was 'terrified' of it. He told me that he had been in the D-day Invasion Force and he had seen a lot of dying. One day he remarked, rather poetically I thought: 'You know, one's Company comes to feel to one like one's own body, and any loss is like the loss of a part of oneself.'

On another day he described that for him the lowering of the body into the grave is the worst moment in a funeral service. And, continuing to discuss death, he remarked with much emphasis: 'I enjoy life, I am greedy for life.' And he thought of death as a punishment and a persecution. Talking about his brother-in-law's death he would ask: 'Why should he have died? He was so good. Too good. It was unjust.' And then he began to express the feeling that perhaps his brother-in-law's death was really his sister's fault. She had sort of killed him. She did not allow him to be a man.

During this time, when the theme of death dominated the analysis, the patient became depressed and gastric symptoms re-appeared. He then told me about a nightmare that had recurred ever since his childhood:

> I am in a cathedral; it is bigger than the biggest cathedral. I am as if weightless. But then, from the front something comes towards me, irrevocably . . . or I am drawn to it . . . irrevocably.

Having told me this nightmare, he then remembered a film he had seen as a child, the German film *Metropolis*. He could only remember a single shot of it—of a huge face, with a huge mouth that sucked people in and emitted flames. He had been so frightened by that part of the film that he had to be taken out of the cinema.

The phase of preoccupation with death and with his war experiences was followed closely by an increased and now eroticised transference. He expressed this in a greedy demand for my love and my concern for him.

The theme of death, followed by the expression of greed, then seemed to provoke phantasies of murderous attacks on the mother's body. He had a dream:

> I drive against the red light into a main road; this causes a lorry to swerve; it loses control, crashes through the various bay windows of a row of houses and finally penetrates into a house, where a woman in bed is seriously injured by it—her belly is ripped wide open.

Shortly after this dream he became hypomanic. He was restless, could not sleep, felt he could not control his anger, feared madness, feared death; there was no euphoria. But—the gastric symptoms disappeared again.

I understood this sequence of events, themes and feelings as follows. Once he had been able to verbalise and to expose himself more consciously to his fear of death he could then become aware of his greed for life—life being symbolised by some of our earliest experiences of it: food, mother and love. But his greed provoked guilt and he expected to be punished for it. The hypomanic restlessness seemed to express his feeling that he was caught in a vicious circle. He felt chased by death; he chased the anti-death, the feeding mother; but then came the fear that his greed would actually damage her and she would punish and revenge herself on him, by killing him.

In the case of Fred there was a relatively well-developed ego, constellated and invested with affect. But he could not feel safe about himself; greed and guilt threatened the fabric of his selfhood. Consequently death was experienced by him as that which destroys, isolates and deprives.

Summing up these three cases, I would say that Clare had hardly moved beyond the stage of the original self; the ego was weak and uncathected; hence death was welcome. Patrick, on the other hand, had invested ego-consciousness with sufficient emotional value so that he had come to fight for its existence, even though he could only do so by such primitive and magical methods as identification with the engulfing and death-giving mother. Fred's ego structure was the most developed of these three patients, though it was not quite solid and firm enough for him to experience the forces and images from the self with anything but fear and hostility.

These three cases thus support my contention that when ego consciousness is experienced as a painful burden and when it seeks for its own destruction, then death is welcome. But when the ego is valued, though experienced as precarious and fragile in relation to the unifying trends of the self, then death is the enemy.

I must, however, stress that I do not regard the death wish as necessarily neurotic, although if either the need to undo separateness or the need for wholeness is compulsive then it is very likely to act as a regressive force leading to neurosis or psychosis. Yet the death wish may also be experienced when the ego is normally strong; for, according to Bellak's definition of a strong ego, there is then available enough energy and confidence to permit the 'self-exclusion of the ego for purposes of creativity and ad hoc needs'. This seems to have been so in the case of those poets and artists who have been particularly aware of the longing for death and self-annihilation.

Fingering through an anthology of poetry I found it more difficult to find poems that mourned the coming of death than poems that welcomed it. Walt Whitman's carol, for example: 'Come, lovely and soothing death . . .' seems to represent centuries of poetic feeling.

One must, of course, be careful, when one examines the

attitude to death in any particular individual, to distinguish the genuine wish for surrender and non-being, that is the genuine longing for the oceanic experience, from a fear of life, a running away from life.

When a neurotic fears death and regards it as a threat to his precariously balanced ego, then he often attempts to opt out of time. One of the ways in which he tries to do this is by refusing to move, to change, to grow. He seems indeed intent on arresting time, as if magically. Thus the fear of dying is often at the root of the fight against change.

In consequence the repetition compulsion, which is really a ritualised stubborn refusal to change and which Freud had regarded as an expression of the death instinct, could also be regarded as a *defence* against the death instinct. And, as is well-known, there is no more powerful obstacle to therapeutic work than the fear of change and the fear of consciousness. The neurotic and the psychotic do truly hold up to us our essential dilemma: to move and to change means to accept awareness of our approaching end. *But* to refuse change means being dead *now*. Awareness of this paradox, of this dilemma, inevitably makes an analyst more sensitive to some of the conflicts that underlie the patient's resistance to the analytic process. But it also helps him to appreciate the courage that he demands of his patient—the courage to relinquish the past, in order to expose himself to life, to change and to uncertainty, which means also to death.

Awareness of his mortality confronts a man with the fact that everything is impermanent. It is a fact that is emphasised in many religions, but it looms particularly large in Buddhist thought. It has led the Buddha to seek a way out of the problem of pain, to which impermanence exposes all creatures, by enjoining on his followers that they attempt to detach themselves and to sever their emotional links to a world that is basically unstable. The disturbed and mentally ill may want to try out just such a solution. How often have I not heard remarks like: 'Why should I get fond of so-and-so? He (or she) will only leave me again.'

Similarly, the analysand may express an angry distrust of the analyst because, as some have said, quite unambiguously, one day analysis will end. In other words, they cling to the fact that they can have their analyst only as long as they are ill, helpless and dependent. Getting better is therefore felt as dangerous. At this stage the patient simply cannot imagine that a time may come when he will need his analyst much less, or perhaps not at all. But even if the patient has come to trust that the analyst will not deliberately forsake him while he, the patient, is still in need of him, yet he may still remain haunted by the possibility that the analyst may have an accident, or get ill or even die. 'No,' as one has said, 'it is better to feel nothing— even if I cannot break the "habit" of coming for my analytic sessions.'

In the case of such patients, sessions may remain charged with a tantalising conflict and the whole of life, so one discovers, is experienced by them as a vast network of contradictions. They do what, apparently, they do not feel, and they feel something that is at odds with what they do.

The difference between the practising Buddhist and the sick person is that the latter is filled with anger, rage, despair and resentment at the frustrations of life, and he refuses to become attached to anything or anybody or even to become aware when he has in fact become attached and dependent on something or somebody. Yet only after a man has experienced attachment and the knowledge and awareness of his attachment, can he attempt to moderate, to reduce and to truly and genuinely sacrifice attachment. The neurotic attempts a short cut—he attempts to remain unaware of his inevitable and necessary dependences. As a result he remains, inevitably, much more helplessly dependent.

But once more I must ask: is the hypothesis of a death drive really necessary or valid or even useful in connection with the examination of man and his relationship to mortality?

An answer that comes to me is that so far man has adjusted to the fact that he is mortal, and that he knows that he is mortal. When I say that man has, on the whole, adjusted to this fact of his existence, I mean that in spite of his awareness of his own mortality, he has succeeded in living out his life, in creating more life by making and having children, and in facing death, when it comes in a more or less prepared and dignified manner. There are even occasions when a man—or woman—is ready to expose himself to death—even to choose death—for the sake of the future, for the survival of his offspring, for the people he loves, or in order to safeguard some beliefs to which he feels committed. In other words, men have not, on the whole, fallen victim to incapacitating depressions, to panic states or to paralysing inaction because of death and of their knowledge of it. Nor have they all needed to develop belief in a *personal* survival, which would, or could be said to, obviate the painful fear of personal extinction. How can we explain such resilience in the face of the knowledge of death, if we do not postulate the existence of some collaborative and preparatory force within man, which enables him to accomplish his biological functions: to live; to learn; to develop to the very edge of his potentialities; and then to disappear again, in order to make room, and so create the possibility of more and even greater development?

If we postulate the existence of Eros, the life force, in order to account for man's need to live, to survive, to procreate and to experience fear when in danger and anger when threatened, how can we explain that he can die without going mad, and that he can live, knowing that he will die—unless we postulate a second and complementary force, Thanatos, the death drive.

There is another reason why a death drive hypothesis seems to me to be so essential; it is because I consider man's need to create as also quite fundamental. But creation itself depends, much more than had been realised until recently, on the continuous interaction of life and death, of activity and passivity, of consciousness and unconsciousness, of assertion and surrender. I hope to be able to show and illustrate this in later chapters.

CHAPTER 3

On the threshold of death: a pilot study of four dying patients

Am I really justified in talking about the predominance of Thanatos—that is, the drive towards death—when I describe those psychological states that are characterised by the experience of fusion, of non-being and of an absence of boundaries? I believe I am, because recent researches on people who are in the process of actually dying suggest that there is indeed a considerable similarity between the psychological states of those who are actually and physically dying and those whose psychic organisation has come under the dominance of the death wish.

As I have already pointed out, psychologists—and I use this term for all who study mental phenomena in all conceivable contexts—have for a long time paid little attention to man's relationship to death, to his attitudes towards it and to the experiences he might have when faced with death as an imminent possibility. In his book *The meaning of death*, published in 1959, Hermann Feifel pointed to this omission:

> Even after looking hard in the literature it is surprising how slim is the systematic knowledge about death. Far too little has been given to assessing thoroughly the implications of the meaning of death.

Since the publication of this book, however, there has in fact been a resurgence of interest in the problem of attitudes to death and the psychology of dying. The researches of, for instance, John Hinton, Robert Kastenbaum, Morton Lieberman, Kubler-Ross, Cecily Saunders, and many others suggest that probably more people become aware when they are nearing death than had been assumed; that many find relief in being able to discuss this more freely than had usually been allowed for; and that indeed quite a large proportion of patients approach their death with a greater degree of acceptance and positive composure than had been expected.

I have been particularly interested in Morton Lieberman's work because his results indicate that 'dying' is really a process extending over several months and involving considerable changes in ego-functioning. On the basis of his results Lieberman has suggested that it is justifiable to regard death not as 'an event', but as a 'process' 'involving true developmental changes during the terminal phase of life.'

Jung, as I have mentioned in the previous chapter, believed that the psyche of man concerns itself spontaneously and naturally with death and with the process of dying, particularly in the second half of life, and that 'it is just as neurotic in old age not to focus upon the goal of death as it is in youth to repress phantasies which have to do with the future.'

In support of his belief that the psyche prepares for death as well as for growth and development, Jung describes his clinical experience as follows:

> I have observed a great many people whose unconscious psychic activity I was able to follow into the immediate presence of death. As a rule the approaching end was indicated by those symbols which, in normal life also, proclaim changes of psychological condition—rebirth symbols such as change of locality, journeys and the like. I have frequently been able to trace back for over a year, in a dream series, the indications of approaching death, even in cases where such thoughts were not prompted by the outward situation. Dying, therefore, has its onset long before the actual death. Moreover, this often shows itself in peculiar changes of personality, which may precede death by quite a long time.'

In 1935, the psychoanalyst Helene Deutsch also put forward a hypothesis in which she proposed that the act of dying 'peacefully' depends on three emotional conditions:

(a) The silencing of feelings of aggression towards others.
(b) The giving up of the cathexes of the objects of this world—which is nowadays called 'disengagement'.
(c) The disappearance of feelings of guilt.

Helene Deutsch believed that these emotional states and conditions could be attained only through regression to the lower levels of psychic development, so that the dying person can exhibit without guilt or embarrassment the emotional cathexes of his early developmental stages.

It has seemed to me that the hypothesis of an unconscious

preparation for death might lend itself well to some empirical investigation. The projection tests, especially the Rorschach inkblot test, might prove particularly sensitive and valuable in such research, for it yields information about the actual structure of an individual's personality, about the dynamic forces that interact inside him, and also about his conscious and unconscious phantasies and images.

Given my basic hypotheses concerning a death drive as a valence of the self, and the speculations concerning the psyche's potential capacity or tendency to prepare for death, I formulated the following specific questions in the hope that the Rorschach test might provide some answers to them.

(i) Do Rorschach responses provide any evidence that there is a wish for death? Are there any indications that the quality of such a wish or its intensity is affected by the imminent approach of death?

(ii) Are there any signs that the psyche of man prepares itself for death? If this is true one way in which this might show itself is in a loosening of ego functions and in a decreased attachment to ego ideals. A Rorschach record might indicate this through the predominance of certain characteristics of perception and in the choice of the area of the inkblot chosen and attended to, as for instance:

Fewer large detail responses;
Fewer pure form responses;
Looser sequence;
Freer use of phantasy and affectivity.

Another indication may be found in the actual content of the images perceived; for they may contain those which both Freud and Jung have in fact regarded as symbolic of death, or which students of the literature and the iconography of death have teased out of their material. Such images and themes might be:

1. Change, growth, transformation.
2. Union and fusion.
3. Bridges, roads, travel, distance.
4. Caves, tunnels, earth, water.

(iii) Do Rorschach records of dying persons provide signs of the ego's defensive reaction to an impending threat of death?

47

Such reactions may take the form of panic, of anxiety and depression, or they may assume a paranoid flavour. The Rorschach signals of such reactions lie in the nature and the quality of the actual perceptual process, in those qualities of the inkblot which a person has actually reacted to; but much of it may also show itself in the images themselves. They may, for instance, revolve around themes like:

1. Trees without roots, branches that are cut off or broken or mutilated objects;
2. Themes of clasping, or of hanging on to something;
3. Themes of drowning, being buried, sucked into something, being invaded or penetrated by hostile objects or forces;
4. Paranoid themes;
5. Sado-masochistic themes.

   (Feifel had found that mental patients more often than normal persons depict death as occurring by violent means.)

The four people used in this pilot study were each suffering from some fatal illness. All, except for Miss B., of whom I lost track, died within fifteen months of my seeing them. Although I did not select them on the basis of whether they were consciously aware of their situation, I tried to assess this as best I could. Two of them, Mr L. and Mr W., a plumber and a farm labourer respectively, were relatively uneducated. Mr J. had a village store in Wales; but he had at one time left his Welsh village in order to study art in one of the big towns in the Midlands. Only Miss B., a short-term patient in a mental hospital, had had higher education and had been to university.

Results

All four patients gave expansive and lengthy records. They seemed to enjoy the opportunity to deploy their imagination. In the case of two of them, Mr L. and Mr W., I had in fact to break the test session into two parts because they became so excited and involved by the test that I feared they might get too tired.

All four subjects attended, more than is usual, to small and even to very small areas of the inkblot, and all of them showed, through an under-emphasis on pure form, that they were not much concerned with the intellectual aspect of the task, nor with the need to control their responses, whether to their inner or their outer world. Instead, they tended to react spontaneously in terms of their feelings and phantasies. In fact, their responses to the colours showed that their reactions to emotional situations might become somewhat uncontrolled and exaggerated. Moreover, there were signs that they were liable to reject and to avoid the more usual and expected emotional reactions and to experience instead emotions in situations that most other people would regard as of little emotional impact. (They often responded to the black, white and grey areas in terms of their colours; Mr W., for instance, used a very small white area on Card I and described it as 'an ulcer' because 'all that is white in the body is an illness'.) It is possible that this tendency to react emotionally to situations that most other people regard as relatively neutral is what creates the emotional isolation of the dying person and to which Eissler has drawn attention in his book, *The psychiatrist and the dying patient.*

In all four records the apperceptions were often fluid and constantly changing; this also confirms the impression that for these subjects the ego's function of reality-testing had become less important than the emotional and imaginary events that were going on inside them.

All of them produced a great many oral responses—that is, responses concerned with food and drink.

These particular characteristics lend support to Helene Deutsch's suggestion that in the process of dying men tend to 'regress to lower levels of psychic development' and that emphasis on ego functions may be sacrificed.

As I was working on these records, my attention was caught by the tendency on the part of all four subjects to produce images that involved either a spatial or a temporal distance. This struck me as an interesting fact deserving further exploration, particularly as Hoffman in an essay on 'Mortality and modern literature', which is included in Feifel's *The meaning of death*, points out that descriptions of death scenes in literature often refer to the experience of an expanding space and to a sense of spaciousness. It is indeed a feasible hypothesis that the imminence of death might well affect profoundly a person's experience of space and of time; the sense of 'experienced' time, for instance, may narrow so that the distant past and the distant future may come to seem to be closer to 'today'. The Rorschach test may thus prove a helpful tool for a phenomenological study of the experience of time and space.

Dealing now with each of these four patients separately, I shall describe some of the relevant historical facts and then discuss in some detail the content of their responses.

Mr W. was a fifty-three-year-old German-born farm labourer. He was his parents' seventh and youngest child. At the age of seven he went to live with a childless uncle and aunt whose home was within sight of his own parents' house. His uncle and aunt were farmers and he started work with them when he was seventeen years old until he joined the army when war broke out. He settled in Wales after a period of internment as a prisoner of war in Texas. In Wales he went back to farm work; in 1948 he married an Irish woman and had three children by her.

In December 1960 Mr W. underwent an operation for an extensive carcinoma of the stomach. When I saw him there were already signs of secondaries; he weighed just over six stone, was unable to work, but pottered around in the house and garden as much as he could manage. He had been told that the operation had been for ulcers; but his wife knew the correct diagnosis. It was not easy to assess how aware he was of the seriousness of his illness. He spoke a lot about the changes he had observed in his body, but his attitude towards them would shift rapidly from hopelessness to denial.

When he was given the test his responses to the first card were pretty morbid and betrayed immediately fear, concern and anxiety about his illness. He saw a woman, a dead woman without a head and an executioner on either side of her. This was followed by 'an ulcer', then 'a neckbone' and finally a quite indefinite perception of 'illness'. His own illness seemed thus to be experienced by him as a persecution both from within and from without.

But the next card showed a sudden change of mood and we find there now a theme of fusion, the joining of 'two loving dogs'.

On Card III he saw the usual two persons in movement, but his own response had an almost orgiastic homosexual quality—he saw 'two men doing rock and roll' and he laughed.

On Card IV, the Father card, he perceived a mysterious

and frightening animal, with big feet but which is actually at a great distance from us here in Great Britain, both spatially and temporally—he saw 'the Abominable Snowman'. Was he trying to ridicule it—so as to contain his fears—when he described it as 'scratching itself'? Apparently Mr W. was rather patriarchal at home, though very dependent upon his wife.

There was a fascinating and unusual twist to Mr W's description of the popular 'bat' response on Card V; for he described the bat as 'a very good animal because it catches insects and so on'. Perhaps insects represented for Mr W. agents of the process of dissolution and, in as much as he fights against dying, a creature that devours these insects is experienced by him as his ally and friend. Such an interpretation was reinforced by a later response to Card VIII, where he described 'an empty fruit, it is the fruit the animals have left; they have eaten it'. Insects, according to Jung, symbolise the unconscious thoughts that threaten to destroy the ego, just as actual insects destroy the body.

Mr W. produced a response to Card VI, the phallic card, that seemed deeply symbolical and rich in meaning. He saw a 'creature, a sort of mussel or oyster, which may,' he said, 'have a diamond inside. It is asleep at the bottom of the sea, but if it were threatened it would close up tightly, and you could not open it.' Indeed, such a creature with a protective shell around its precious and indestructible core would be truly invulnerable to 'insects'.

The Mother card provoked a frankly sexual image of the female genitals. A little later he could see the usual women, but he saw them as aggressively fighting each other over 'something'. They were distanced in time—'they are in a very old century and their hair-style is of the seventeenth century'. Would it be too far-fetched to suspect here an unconscious allusion to the woman as the Goddess of Death whom Freud in his essay, 'The theme of the three caskets', identifies as the third of the three Spinners of Fate?

The last three cards of the Rorschach are all coloured cards, and this seems to have made Mr W. think of the tropics. That is indeed a region of teeming life and of a speeded-up life-cycle. The same association occurred to Mr L., as I shall describe later.

I have already mentioned Mr W's major response to Card

VIII—'the empty fruit'. On Card IX Mr W. saw a tree from which dropped into a jar a substance that 'makes the hair grow' and 'which has a good smell'. This is surely a magical substance, rejuvenating and life-giving.

Finally, on Card X Mr W. saw a dangerous creature—'one bite from it and you can die; how do you call it—a scorpion? No, a kind of spider—well, these are eating. You see, here is a mouth; it closes like that' (he snapped his own mouth shut), 'and it has finished these; it will turn to eat these next.' Then he saw 'underground rocks' which, he said, made 'a good hiding place', then followed the perception of two dogs guarding the entrance; then 'water', and finally he wove all these images together into a single image of 'a crossing through the sea': 'You go in through here, you cross the water, and you pass out there'. (He passed his hand through the usual caterpillars at the bottom of the card and brought it to the top of the card.) This is, of course, an image of death, that we find in many cultures and religions.

My second case, Mr L., was a man of sixty-four, a plumber, married and with children, who had had five myocardial infarcts. He had been admitted to a mental hospital in an acute toxic confusional state, the result of a sixth infarction, but he had emerged from this by the time he was tested. He was a bit voluble and reminisced a good deal; he knew he would never be able to work again.

Mr L. saw a vague form only in the first card: 'seaweed'. This led him to talk about the deep, dark sea and then he told me at length about a seaweed collection which had been given to him by his aunt; he had added to this and later he, in his turn, had passed it on to his son. This seaweed collection was thus something of an heirloom, which transcended the generations and yet linked them one to the other.

On Card III Mr L. saw 'two old-fashioned flunkeys arguing over a bird or a turkey'. There is probably an oral element in the image of the turkey. But birds as such play an important part in folklore and mythology and usually represent the soul. In Egyptian hieroglyphs, for instance, a bird was represented by the same sign as 'Ba', the soul—the soul that flies away from the body at death. As a last response to this card Mr L. saw 'a snail with its shell on its back', perhaps expressing through this image his need to feel safe and always 'at home'.

His responses to the Father, the phallic and the Mother cards were relatively flat and dull and he tended to shrink away from the blots as a whole and instead clung to small and unconnected areas, though he himself was uncomfortable with this bittiness. Actually when handed Card VII, the Mother card, Mr L. had become more enterprising and had begun for the first time to turn a card. He then returned to his initial image to the first card, the pressed seaweed.

Card VIII, the first all-coloured card, evoked numerous and most interesting responses. There were 'frogs' and 'chameleons' —both animals that undergo transformation. Then there was the 'old sower'—who was also seen as 'a monk with a shaven head'—and 'he is sowing seed on the ground; it looks a bit like rocky ground; I think it represents agriculture or birth. But the birds are picking up the seed and are scattering it into the distance.' And then he saw 'a man and a lady', walking arm in arm; 'they enjoy this walk; they walk into the distance'. And then he linked all these images together and perhaps he attempted to immortalise them when he described them as forming a coat-of-arms.

On Card IX there seemed to be a change of mood and the theme of loss predominated—he saw an 'orchid, severed from its stem', or 'a peach split open' and 'two golden plums, cut in half, the stone has been taken out of the centre'.

On Card X Mr L. saw 'beetles attacking this stalk, hanging on to it and eating their way into it. I am gastronomic in my choices.' Maybe Mr L's beetles have the same meaning as the 'insects' seem to have had for Mr W., the insects that 'eat their way into the fruit', devour it and so bring about its dissolution.

In nature the birth of one usually demands the death of the other and Mr L. did indeed seem to feel this truth very deeply inside him, as is shown by his last response, which he described with much excitement:

> And this is ivy. It is hanging on. It is a creeping plant. It hangs on in the jungle. It grows. It shoots out shoots and then attaches itself in some manner to what is nearest; and then these reproduce again, and this sets off a new cycle. And when it falls it will seed, because then it is fertile and ready for seeding and so it starts a new cycle of life. It is like vine.

And, like Mr W., Mr L. interpreted the colourfulness of the last card as representing 'the tropics'. Four of the seven responses to this last card deal with the image of a tree to which cling animals and plants. I wonder if the tree symbolised for Mr L. the tree of life to which we cling for a short time, to which we add and from which we then disappear'? If this is so, then there may be a symbolic link between the trees on this card, the coat-of-arms on Card VIII and the seaweed collection on Cards I and VII.

Mr J., the third subject, was a man of fifty-four, who suffered from diabetes and had been in two serious diabetic comas. He was the third child and only boy of poor Welsh parents. He had felt that his mother had been possessive and that his father had been distant and lacking in understanding. He had wanted to be an artist and in fact had managed to get through art school on scholarships. But in the end he returned to Wales and helped to run the family's village store. He married at the age of fifty-one an English girl of thirty-four who was partly crippled from polio. Unlike the first two patients, Mr J. had in the past suffered from neurotic conflicts and maladjustments. But in spite of initial impotence in his marriage he did succeed in fathering a baby.

Already, on Card I there were signs of ambivalence about being and non-being. There were images of 'a person drowning', of 'a couch' that gives him the feeling of being 'engulfed', but there are also themes of retreat into containment in his perception of the pelvis and the harbour; and there was an ecstatic surrender to boundless excitement, when he saw a person singing for joy and music going up, 'music sweeps up'.

His disinterest in control and boundaries was shown again on Card II, where he described the coloured area as conveying 'joy'; the red gave him 'the feeling of joy, jumping for joy; there is a feeling of exultation'. And then he described seeing 'sexual intercourse . . . there is excitement; it is the climax'. And again he saw 'music which sweeps up'. I have been wondering whether Mr J.'s emphasis on sound, on music, might be understood as a defence against silence, which Freud has regarded as another symbol of death when it appears in dreams. Mr J.'s response to Card III could be interpreted as concern with the bad and dirty things that may be felt to be inside him and which may cut him off from others and so isolate him. The image of 'the sound of shouting voices; they fade, they disappear into the distance', is followed by the image of 'somebody, a man, is using a chamber pot'.

54

Card IV created, in quick oscillations, both horror, fear of death and signs of dependency and a need for love and fusion. Thus, the 'monster that encloses you' and 'death and agony' are followed by 'soft fur', and 'a swan and a figure bending over it . . . I hear music and have a feeling of green', and they in turn were followed by 'a vampire' and 'clouds after a storm'.

On Card V there was evidence that the regressive needs for fusion and withdrawal continued to predominate. Again he saw 'a harbour'; then a woman with 'prominent breasts' and finally a 'rabbit who is hurrying, going down a hole'.

The phallic card provoked concern with food and fear of the angry, the scolding woman.

The Mother card showed quite unequivocally his wish to surrender to the mother for the sake of being able to enjoy peace, containment and security; for he described the 'peacefulness of the night', and 'home and the woman in a white dress and a dark coat' who waited for him.

His responses to Card VIII expressed longing for the great depth, for the 'cushion of indolence and easy living' but these longings were counterbalanced by thoughts of 'the dreadful scramble', and of 'danger and rocks and ravines'.

On Card IX we observe the progress of a frankly sadomasochistic battle. 'The Spanish Inquisition . . . people in pain'; and there were also overtly paranoid phantasies . . . 'people doing things behind your back. . . .' 'Unseen people watching you' and in the enquiry the 'unseen people watching you' was elaborated into 'father watching me . . . the colours give me this feeling; it is a feeling of peace'. But this then brought him to experience 'a feeling of failure'.

His need for fusion found once more expression on Card X when he had a 'light-as-air feeling' and perceived a 'sexual intercourse in the open air'. But to this is now added 'a feeling of spring time' which 'makes one feel young and happy'.

I had been hesitant about using this record because its psychopathological quality was so marked that other features apart from the imminence of death were obviously involved. This man did, however, after all lead a relatively normal life and his record did show in an extraordinarily clear form the fear and the attraction towards states of being and non-being, and that a person can experience these almost simultaneously.

Miss B., the fourth subject, was an unmarried woman of

thirty-eight. She had been an only child. Her father had been
in the diplomatic service. Both parents had died within a week
of one another in 1948. Both had been Christian Scientists.
Ten years after their death the patient developed a carcinoma
of the breast and underwent excision of the tumour. Another
excision had had to be undertaken in 1961. She then became
depressed and paranoid and was admitted to the mental
hospital.

She seemed to have idealised her parents but described herself as 'a selfish little beast' because she had left her parents
for a time when she had joined the W.R.N.S. during the war.

On Card I the sequence from 'a bat with a small head
tucked inside' to 'an awful black cockroach with its legs waving
in the air' suggests that she probably experienced a close link
between death and the womb.

On Card II she again reacted to the blackness of the card—
and saw 'black puppies'.

On Card III there was a change from an emphasis on illness—'an X-ray showing T.B. spots' and 'a broken branch' to
phantasies of glamour and power—'a robe of office'; 'Bona-
parte's hat' and 'a ruby brooch'.

On the Father card she saw, 'a giant; his hat has come off
somewhere'. In actual fact, shortly after their escape from
France in 1940, her father had had a cerebral haemorrhage,
which had left him paralysed and relatively helpless.

On Card V she saw the usual bat 'hanging on to something';
then, 'a dead bird'; and lastly 'two giants asleep, leaning
against a rabbit'—this last response struck me as a most sad
but realistic self-portrait—the two dead giants, the parents,
leaning against her, the rabbit.

On the Mother card the patient saw 'a human pyramid'. I
have been wondering whether this image might not be the
symbolical equivalent of the 'tree' in Mr L.'s record.

All the coloured cards seemed to evoke a regressive wish to
cling and to fuse with another being.

Thus on Card VIII she saw 'Siamese twins; they have been
dumped in the snow; they are not even crying; they don't
know what has happened to them'.

On Card IX there were 'two lobsters getting out of their
lobster pots; but they cling to their pot, they just can't leave
it'.

And on Card X there were 'bats clinging to each other'. Her very last response, however, seemed to allude to the existence of something permanent and indestructible and it recalled Mr W.'s image of the diamond in the oyster. Miss B. saw here 'stones on the bottom of the sea-bed. They shine like jewels.' This response brought to my mind Ariel's song in *The Tempest*:

> Full fathom five thy father lies
> Of his bones are coral made
> Those are pearls that were his eyes.

Discussion and conclusion

These few Rorschach records seemed indeed to lend weight to the hypothesis that: (1) the wish for life and the wish for death do co-exist in the psyche, and (2) their predominance, relative to one another, is likely to vary according to (a) the state of mental health on the one hand, and (b) the actual nearness to death on the other. Thus all four patients produced some images that seemed to symbolise death, both in its hostile and negative aspect—'empty fruit', 'small deathly creatures', 'severed plants', 'illness', 'threatening persons', 'drowning', 'clinging', etc.—as well as images that seemed to symbolise the idea of the transience of one's personal life and a belief that death is an integral part of life—thus symbols such as 'the tree', 'the old sower', 'the tropics', the 'life-cycle of plants' and 'the sea journey'. These four subjects, who were all nearing death, in fact produced the sort of imagery that students of man's symbolic expression have interpreted as referring to death; furthermore these symbols betrayed attitudes of both resistance and also of surrender to it.

Some of the features of these four records and many of the images produced by these subjects were quite new to me; and they differed markedly from all the records I had obtained and collected while working for several years in a mental hospital. If a larger sample should provide similar results, then this would indeed be important evidence to support the hypothesis that the psyche of man does prepare itself for death irrespective of whether or not he is consciously aware that he is nearing the end of his life.

CHAPTER 4

The birth of death: some African stories

An individual's attitude to death—and this may apply also to the general attitude to death of a whole socio-cultural group—may depend on a position on a 'wholeness-separateness axis'. In other words, if a person's or a group's libido is invested predominantly in the attempt to develop separateness and a personal and well-differentiated identity, then he may be said to lie closer to the separateness end of the proposed axis; in that case he is likely to regard death as the enemy, as the thief, the destroyer. But the person who searches above all for wholeness, union, synthesis—irrespective of whether this is expressed in regressive psychopathological symptoms or in progressive and creative drives—such a person is likely to look upon death as liberator, as bringer of peace and union.

We may advance another step further our understanding of the complexity of the thoughts and feelings men have about death through a study of the myths of the origin of death in the world.

All over the world and among most people there is the story that originally men did not die. Instead they either stayed eternally the same, or else they went through cycles of youth, age, and then rejuvenation or resurrection. But then according to all these stories, there was an event, something happened that allowed death to slip into the world and so made man its victim.

For a long time both anthropologists and psychologists have been intrigued by the almost universal presence of such myths. The basic contents of these myths are remarkably similar. Their form is poetic and imaginative, awesome and symbolic. They express unobservable realities in terms of observable phenomena. Through a story of a time 'long, long ago', which tells of people, of their relationship to one another and of the actions they do or fail to do, the myths attempt to explain problems such as the origin of the world, life and death, social institutions, cosmic events, man's place in the universe and the possible meaning of it all. Indeed, Jung and many other students of mythology have suggested that it is the rôle and the function of myths to give to men security and inner strength so that they do not feel crushed by the mysteriousness and inexorability of the universe. For men do need to find some sense in their lives and so they seek to discover the meaning of the world.

Through the study of these myths one can often discover the more general and sometimes also the more unconscious beliefs, needs, fears and hopes of men, in terms of themselves as individuals and as members of a community; and through these myths they often express their ideas of good and bad, right and wrong, real and unreal.

The sort of incidents that have supposedly rendered mankind vulnerable to death reveal much similarity of thought and also considerable overlap of moral values. Be it in the Americas, in Africa, Australia, Asia or Europe, we tend to find origin of death stories based on only a small number of similar themes. This being so I have decided to concentrate on a study of African myths; for there exists an excellent collection of them assembled and published by Abrahams in 1951. His researches have proved a most valuable source. As I read them I found myself enchanted by their poetic insights and by the remarkable psychological awareness that seems inherent in them. They challenge one to seek an understanding of their various and subtle implications.

Like the origin of death myths in other parts of the world, some of the African myths express themes with which we in the West are also relatively familiar. But there are others that seem almost inconsequential. These myths about the origin of death offer us not only more clues about man's thoughts and feelings about life and death, but they also comment on man's relationship to the dead, to the living, to God, to sin and to existence in the world.

As I read through them I found that on the basis of an analysis of their themes, the African myths could be divided up into four major groups:

In the first group are myths—very common and widely

59

distributed all over Africa, but also widespread among North American Indian tribes—in which two or more animals carry the messages of death and of immortality between God and men. For one reason or another—and I shall enumerate some of them later on—the message of death arrives first and so establishes the natural order of things.

The second group is made up of those myths whose central theme is closely akin to the 'Paradise Lost' story of the Judeo-Christian tradition. Consequently this is more familiar to us. Here death is thought of as having been imposed on man— usually by God, but occasionally by an angry or offended animal—as a punishment for disobedience, or a misdemeanour; or else it has been introduced as a way of checking man's attempt to rival God.

The third group is of quite particular interest to me, because it consists of a considerable number of stories in which men themselves overtly and deliberately choose death.

Finally, there are a few stories, mainly from Madagascar, that describe death as a way of keeping open the communication between God and man. These stories are indeed very beautiful; I regard them as a sensitive expression of man's great need to explore and to bring into relationship with one another the heaven, the earth and the underworld that lie inside him.

Group I: Animal messengers

1. God gave the dog a medicine that would restore life to people who had been killed by the Toucan—the slayer of men. The dog had not far to go, but en route he found a bone and put the medicine down and began to gnaw the bone. The goat, passing by, took the medicine and poured it over its people, the grass. When the dog had finished eating he could not find the medicine, so he returned to God. But God could not now do anything about the matter. 'That is why to this day men die and do not return, but grass which dies every year comes back again.' (From the Kraci)

2. God told the chameleon to tell men that they would never die; but the creature found sweet berries on the way and forgot his message. God became angry and despatched the lizard to tell men that they should die. The lizard delivered the mes-

sage. Then the chameleon arrived, but the people laughed at him and his message. 'We have heard the opposite story from the lizard and we believe him,' they said. (From the Swazi)

3. Men formerly did not die, but lived as slaves. When they grew tired of their slavery they sent their friend, the dog, to God asking him to end these intolerable conditions. The dog passed an old woman who was boiling something, and believing it was food the dog stayed. Meanwhile the goat came by and having heard the message the dog was to deliver, decided to convey it herself. The dog continued the journey, when he saw the woman was only boiling water. He then met the goat who told him that she had told God that men were tired of their slavery and wished to die. The dog hurried to God to rectify things, but God would not listen to him, for He had already arranged that men should die. That is why death comes to all men and men remain slaves. (From the Dagomba)

4. A great man sent the chameleon to God to ask whether when a man is dead and buried, everything is then finished, or if, after a few days, medicine is trickled into his eyes, would he then rise from the dead? But the chameleon went so slowly that a toad was sent with the same question and arrived before the chameleon. God felt unpleasantly affected by both the question and the disgusting animal, so He said that when men died everything was at an end, one could only lament and bury him. And when the chameleon arrived God said it should be as He had said to the toad. This is why men die and do not return to life. (From the Baja-Kaka)

5. God gave man the choice 'whether the moon, when it has died, shall disappear for ever, or whether human beings who have died shall pass away for all time'. After counsel, the dog and goat were sent to God to say that men who have died should return but that the moon should disappear for ever. But the goat stopped by the wayside to eat, so the dog reached God first and said that men wished to pass away for ever and that the moon should rise again. When the goat came with the right answer, God said, 'Go away. It shall be as the dog has said.'

There is a postscript to this story, which tells us that God came afterwards to earth and punished the dog and the goat who had previously been human beings. He threw a throwing stick at them after which they went on all fours. (From the Bongo)

6. The Creator knew that Life and Death, wrapped in a grass-cloth, tied to a pole as for burial, would be coming along the road to try to reach men. So he charged the dog and the goat to watch by the roadside and allow Life to pass, but not Death. The two animals quarrelled as to which would be the most suitable sentinel, the dog asserting that he would stay awake while the goat considered the dog would fall asleep at his post. After a time the goat went away and left the dog to watch. The dog made a fire, but then went to sleep. Then Death got past. Next day the goat kept watch. He stayed awake and captured Life. Thus Death was allowed to reach men on account of the dog's negligence, while Life had been captured. And people said, 'If God had watched, Death would have been caught.' (From the Luba)

7. God sent for the chameleon and told him that when a man dies one should touch him with bread and he would come back to life. But the lizard heard this and quickly ran to the humans and said, 'When a man dies, you should bury him.' The chameleon took his time, putting on fine clothes and embellishing his head with blue dye. When he finally reached men with his message, they said, 'Which ever comes first is King.' (From the Hausa)

8. Men were asked whether they desired that the dead should return or not. They sent the chameleon with the answer that they wished them to return, but when the chameleon had gone, they changed their minds and sent a message to God with the lizard, who was to ask Him to let the women live and the men die, or if this were not possible to let all die. The lizard reached God long before the chameleon and God granted her request. (From the Cwana)

9. God threw a broken calabash into the water and said to the tortoise, 'Just as the broken calabash returns to the land so shall man, when he dies, later return to life. Go and tell men this.' But the tortoise threw a stone into the water and said, 'Just as the stone returns never more, so the people, when they are dead, shall never more return to life.' When the tortoise's father died, he was buried according to God's instructions; but when the tortoise asked Him when her father was coming back

God said, 'Never, because that is what you told the people. You had changed my message.' (From the Dahomey)

While trying to account for the origin of death, these stories also tell us something of a people's attitude to sin and to instinctual indulgences. Clearly the various animal messengers act as convenient projection-screens and in the case of one or two stories awareness of this is almost explicit. The postscript to the story told by the Bongo, for instance, tells that the animals had originally been people, but that God had turned them into animals as a punishment for having bungled the message.

A survey of the various 'sins' laid at the door of these animals and held responsible for the introduction of death shows that there are five principal ones. They are:

(i) Greed.
(ii) Sleepiness.
(iii) Narcissism or vanity.
(iv) Laziness, tardiness, slowness—in other words variants on sloth.
(v) Hatred of men.

The animals chosen most often as the carriers of either the message of death or the message of immortality tend to be the small and rather harmless creatures, such as the chameleon, the lizard, the goat, the sheep, the dog, the hare, the tortoise, the frog and the toad. But their rôles are by no means fixed, nor are the characteristics attributed to them invariable. Thus while one culture group selects a particular animal as the carrier of the message of immortality, another culture group chooses the very same animal as the carrier of the message of death. In other words men differ in their feelings about any particular animal; and its symbolic meaning is not necessarily given and static, but is probably affected by other factors also such as geography, history and, above all, ecology. This discovery must necessarily act as a warning against any premature or *a priori* interpretation of animal symbolism.

Group II: The sins of man

This next group of stories—which I have described as more akin to the Judeo-Christian myth—seeks the cause of the coming of death more directly in the faults of men themselves.

1. Men were in the habit of conversing with Imana, the High God. One day Imana said, 'Keep watch; do not sleep tonight; I shall come and bring you good tidings.' A snake which was in the house overheard this. At the first cock-crow the man fell asleep and when Imana called him, he did not answer. But the snake did so in his place. So Imana said to the snake, 'Thou shalt die, but thou shalt arise again; thou shalt become old, but thou shalt get a new skin, thou, thy children and thy children's children.' Next morning the man went to Imana and told Him that he had heard nothing. But the snake had by then been given eternal life and the decision could not be changed. (From the Ruanda)

2. One day the children began to die; so men asked Olurun, the Great God, what was the cause of this. He replied that this had come about because the sons were sleeping with the young women that belonged to the fathers. Since then, so men say, death kills both old and young people. (From the Yoruba)

3. Formerly no one needed to die. One day God wished to see whether man or snake was worthy of immortality; so He arranged a race between them. During the race the man met a woman and stopped to smoke and chat with her for such a long time that the snake reached God first. So God said to man, 'The snake is worthier than thou; she shall be immortal; but you shall die and all your race.' (From the Gudji and Darasa)

4. At one time people lived to a great age before they died and it is not known why they now live such short lives or who brought death into the world. But it is said that those who had no sons poisoned the sons of others. And so it is said, 'It is not God who kills men, but envy.' (from the Acoli)

5. One day God said to a man that if a child should die he was to say as he threw away the body, 'Man die and come back again; moon die and remain away.' One day a child died, but it was not the man's own, so he threw it away and he said, 'Man die and remain away; moon die and return.' The next time one of his own children died; so as he threw it away he used the first-mentioned formula. But God told him that it could not be used any longer, and that he had forfeited his chance of restoring the child to life by his actions on the previous occasion.

'And this is how it comes about that when a man dies he does not return, but when the moon is finished it comes again and is always visible to us.' (From the Masai)

6. Death did not exist among the first men. One day a chameleon asked a man for a beer jug, crept slowly up the jug and dipped itself in the beer, after which it asked the man to drink it. When the man refused—the chameleon was regarded as venomous and loathsome—the chameleon said, 'From henceforth you shall die.' But the snake, which had obeyed the request to drink the beer, was allowed to live by changing its skin and thus be born anew. (From the Bantu)

7. An old man and his aged wife sent their two children to fetch water. While the latter were away the parents intended to change their skins; but in order that they should have enough time the children were sent to fetch the water in market bags of raffia. Twice they returned with leaking bags and so were sent back; but the third time they stole into the house just as their parents were half out of their old skins. So the father cried to them, 'Now you see me as I am. Shall I now burst like a pot, or shall I burst like a calabash, which can be mended?' The son desired the former, so the father burst and died. (From the Wadchugga)

8. God originally lived with human beings, who were ignorant of pain and death. When they grew old they spent nine days near a little tree called Singe and so were rejuvenated and began life anew. But the people became wicked and forgot to reverence God. So God told the people to break a bundle of sticks that were tied together, but no one succeeded until God himself had undone the bundle. 'You see,' said God, 'the advantage of union. Why have you all forsaken me? As a punishment I shall withdraw far away from you. You will all be different one from the other and all of you, men, women and children, will know suffering and death.' (From the Koko)

The main faults and failings of men that the African has singled out as so important and serious as to lead to the origin of death make up a fairly formidable list. All such failings are really what one might regard as 'original sin' and was it not original sin that, according to the Hebrews, led to the 'Fall' and hence to death?

Reading through this group of stories—those that I have recounted here as well as those I have had to leave out—I have arrived at a list of eight such 'original sins'. They are:

- (i) Greed.
- (ii) Sleep.
- (iii) Curiosity.
- (iv) Impatience.
- (v) Hatred, jealousy, envy, rivalry and the conflicts among men.
- (vi) Disobedience.
- (vii) Lack of reverence for the Great God.
- (viii) The eating of the forbidden fruit—or of the sacred, the forbidden animal. This is often considered as evidence that man desires to make himself the equal of God. This particular type of prohibition is very likely connected with the suppression of ceremonial cannibalism, and of the 'totemic feast' as conceived and described by Freud.

This African list of 'sins' agrees in many respects with our own moral values. In a list based on the Judeo-Christian tradition, however, it is the sexual misdemeanours that figure very much more prominently; but these are in fact quite absent from the African code. On the other hand, the inclusion of 'sleep' as a great sin may seem to us a strange and unexpected addition, though it has already featured in the list I made from the myths in Group I. The only allusion in the Judeo-Christian mythology to the sin of sleep that occurs to mind is Christ's mild reproach to the disciples when they could not resist sleep while he was sorely troubled in the garden of Gethsemane.

If one compares this list of human sins with the list of animal sins, one is struck by the fact that the human sins are rather more comprehensive. They encompass the animal, that is the instinctive, sins like greed and sleep, but then more failings are added, like curiosity and impatience. These qualities are particularly crucial to man's psychic growth, to his development of greater mastery of the world around him and to a deeper consciousness within; this then broadens his general awareness and increases his capacity to resist the need for the immediate satisfaction of his needs, so that he can later on fulfil them more adequately and completely. Such capacity is of necessity based on an enlarged perspective of time. The other 'sins' in the list, such as disobedience, jealousy, envy and rivalry with God, refer to the relationships established, and believed to be desirable, between men and men, men and nature and men and God; they depend on definite beliefs—which may be explicit or implicit—about man's place in his society and in the universe.

Group III: Man 'chooses' death

1. God let the people choose between two mats: one the mat of captivity, the other the mat of death. They rejected the mat of captivity and when they lay down upon the other, they began to die. (From the Dogon)

2. God asked men if they wanted to live for ever or die. They replied that the earth was growing full of people and it would be better if some would die to make room for those who were to come. God agreed. (From the Nuer)

3. In the beginning men did not die, but grew to an immense size, then shrank and finally turned into stones. But there came to be so many old people that men prayed to God to free them from long life, and so death came. (From the Yoruba)

4. Formerly men had no fire but ate all food raw. When they died, God made them young again. One day they hit upon the idea of begging God for fire. But God said to the man who had come to convey the message that He would give him fire if he was prepared to die. The man took fire from God; but since that time all men must die. (From the Darasa)

5. God created men healthy and strong and could not understand why they became cold and stiff. One day He met Death and asked him if he was the cause. Death said he would show God that the people themselves asked for him. God concealed Himself behind a banana tree and waited and an old slave came along, bewailing his lot, saying, 'Oh, the dead are well off. If only I had never been born.' He at once fell down dead. Then came an old woman complaining about her troubles and she, too, fell down dead. Death said: 'Do you see?' And God went away, saddened since His creatures called upon death. (From the Bamum)

6. Originally men did not wage war with one another. No one died of illness or anything else. But a woman called

Muamba, with her son Kalala, came from afar to see the country and on the way they met black ants that had been waging war and now returned bringing with them white ants. Kalala said: 'I too want to make war, like these ants, and kill men.' His mother said laughingly that he might as well begin with her. And so Kalala dug a grave by the side of the path and he buried his mother alive. (From the Tumbwe)

7. One day a little man with two bundles, one big, one small, came to a man who was working in the forest and told him to choose one of them. 'This one,' he said, taking the big bundle, 'contains looking-glasses, knives, beads, cloth, etc. and this,' indicating the small bundle, 'contains everlasting life.' But the man did not venture to choose for himself, but went to ask other people in the town first. While he was away some women came along and they were told to make the same choice. They tried the edges of the knives, admired themselves in the mirrors and forthwith chose the big bundle. The little man disappeared with the other bundle. When the first man returned he found only the women busy sharing out the contents of the big bundle. But men had now lost eternal life, and death remained on the earth. And this is why the people say, 'Oh, if those women had only chosen the small bundle, we folk would not be dying like this'. (From the Ngala)

8. God called men and women together and said to them: 'You can choose either to procreate and to die, or to live for ever.' The men wanted to elect to live for ever, but the women were the first to express their desire. 'We want to die . . . we want to bring children into the world and we shall give them the names of those who have died.' The men protested, but it was too late, and the women's request was granted. (From the Evee)

9. In order that the human couple, whom God had sent to earth, might not become the equal of God they were forbidden to work and to procure food for themselves. They ate with God and came to Heaven when a bell rang at meal-times—nor were they allowed to live together and produce children, since this would cause them to forget God. But a friend of the woman visited the couple one day and gave them fire and said it was wrong not to till the soil and get one's own food. So the couple forgot God's decree, tilled the soil, ate at their own table and

lived as man and wife. When God met the man, the latter said his wife was ill—in fact, she was pregnant and afterwards bore a son and later a daughter. When God told His own wife what had happened, she caused discord among the children and let death and evil appear among them because their father had done wrong. (From the Efik)

10. God created tortoises, men and stones, a male and female of each species. The tortoises and the human beings were given life, but not the stones. None of them gave birth to children. The tortoise wished to have children and made a request to this effect to God. But God replied that He had given life to tortoises and men, but not permission to beget children. At that time men became very old, but they did not die but were rejuvenated. The tortoise returned and made a second request and God said: 'You still want children? Do you realise that if the living have two or three children they must die?' But both the tortoise and men cherished the same wish and demanded children and then death. But the stones did not want children, nor to die—and so it was decreed. And thus came children and death to the world. (From the Nupe)

11. Once upon a time, when the children were cooking their food on the fire, they would take a stick, push with it and say: 'Great God, give us meat as an addition to our meal.' And the meat would then be sent from heaven. But one day an old woman who was pounding her food, bumped into God and asked Him to step back a little. He complied, but the woman asked Him to step back even further. God went up into the air and He was no longer near at hand. (From the Ashanti)

A perusal of the myths in this group suggests that men can and actually do express a wish for death, but that this wish has two distinct forms. In its first form death is desired, not for oneself but for some other person. In this case, therefore, the introduction of death is the result of the hatred, jealousy, envy, rage and rivalry that people are prone to bear towards one another, and which can be so great that it can drive them to the point of wishing the other dead and gone for ever. The stories of Group III seem to pick out the same sort of human failings as the cause for the arrival of death as do the stories in Group II, with the difference that in Group II these 'sins' provoke the anger of God and so lead to His decision to punish offending mankind with death. In Group III these same sins act as the direct causal agent for the presence of death.

However, once the wish for the death of the other has been voiced, even if only once by one of the 'original' personages, the great God seems to be remarkably willing to allow the hateful passion its way. And so He permits the destructive wish to be accomplished. But—and this comes usually as a shock and a surprise to the first culprit—once God has granted that the wish for the death of the other be fulfilled, He then imposes death on everybody, including him who first expressed the wish.

In its second form, death is desired for everybody—including the petitioner himself. Most of the stories provide a reason or a motif for such a wish and I have found the result of my attempt to categorise these reasons most thought-provoking. Again there seem to be eight major categories:

   (i) The alternative to death—usually the possibility of captivity—is more daunting than death itself. (Has not the person living in the age of nuclear weapons felt himself confronted by a very similar choice?)

  (ii) Without death there would hang over man the threat of overpopulation.

 (iii) Death is the only escape from illness and old age.

  (iv) Some myths speak of a general weariness and disgust with the 'troubles of life' and it is this that tempts men to choose death or to request God for it.

   (v) Without death, so some imply, life would be dull, unadventurous and meaningless.

  (vi) Whereas, in our own creation-myth, work is a punishment that follows the loss of immortality, in some of the African myths it is man who deliberately chooses work, and hence death, rather than immortality.

 (vii) A particularly important theme concerns the need felt by both men and women to beget and to have children. And procreation is almost always and everywhere regarded as incompatible with eternal life.

(viii) Closely connected with this last theme and, as it were, a corollary of it, is expressed the wish and the need of man to renew himself.

We would rather die like banana trees who leave descendants than like the moon who rises again.

Finally, there is Group IV:

Group IV: Mortal men as messengers

Once upon a time God sent down to earth His son to look into everything and advise on the possibility of creating living beings. At his father's orders the son left the sky and came down to the globe of the earth. But it was insufferably hot and he could not live anywhere, and so he plunged into the depths of the earth to find a little coolness. He never appeared again. God waited a long time for His son to return. Uneasy at not seeing him, He sent servants to look for him. They were men who came to earth and each of them went a different way to try to find the missing person. But all their searching was fruitless.

God's servants were wretched, for the earth was almost uninhabitable, it was so dry, so hot, so arid and so bare. Seeing the uselessness of their efforts, men sent from time to time one of their number to inform God of the failure of their search and to ask for fresh instructions. Numbers of men were thus despatched back to the Creator, but unluckily not one returned to earth. They are the dead. To this day messengers are still sent to Heaven since the son has not yet been found and no reply from God has reached the earth, where the first men settled and multiplied. They do not know what to do—should they go on looking or should they give up? Alas, not one of the messengers has returned to give us information on this point. And yet we still keep sending them, and the unsuccessful search continues. For this reason it is said that the dead never return to earth. But to reward mankind for their persistence in looking for His son, God sent rain to cool the earth and to allow His servants to cultivate the plants they need for food. (From the Malagasy)

Surely this is one of the most beautiful parables of man's need to search for God and of his anxiety lest he may never accomplish this.

General discussion

Apart from the various animals who deliver the message of death in the first group of myths, Groups II and III point to the belief that it is above all the woman who is responsible for the existence of death or actually chooses it quite deliberately.

This coupling of woman with death, apart from our own Adam and Eve and the serpent story, is almost universal. But the African myths at times make it quite clear why this should be so. For they recognise that a woman wants above all to make and to bear children and that she is therefore least likely to surrender this satisfaction for the sake of immortality. Thus one or two of the African myths tell quite plainly how the original woman had willingly chosen death as the price for her right to bring children into the world.

The African stories use only a limited number of objects as symbols of immortality. There is one instance in which grass is used as such a symbol, but much more often and much more widespread are the myths that use the moon or the snake; their characteristics seem to appeal to men as a suitable representation of eternal life. The moon, as so many of the stories describe, represents the capacity to die and then to return again, unaltered. The snake, on the other hand, is clearly used as a symbol of rejuvenation. A creature that can shed its old skin and then start life again, as it were renewed, is obviously most impressive. The urban European, living in a northern climate, is unlikely to stumble across a shed snake skin and hence he has little direct and tangible experience of this particular 'snaky' quality. No wonder that European and American analysts have been much more preoccupied with the snake's phallic shape and have thus tended to interpet its symbolic significance in this sense only. And no wonder that they have been much more puzzled and much more at a loss to find a satisfactory interpretation and explanation for those who have used the snake as a symbol of wisdom, of healing, of survival and of resurrection.

Of all the stories of the origin of death, the most puzzling, but also the most intriguing, are those in Group I in which an animal messenger bungles or perverts the message. As I have already said, sometimes a motive is ascribed to the animal, sometimes a defect of ability or character is given as the cause. But quite often the story gives no hint at all of any motive or any real reason. This is so particularly in those stories in which the animal himself changes the original message.

The behaviour of God is also rather strange and mystifying in these stories. Why, after all, does He send the two conflicting messages? And why can He not reverse the situation so that it conforms to His original message, even if the wrong or the second message has arrived first?

Again, even the behaviour of men is ambiguous and enigmatic. After all, why should they refuse to accept the message of immortality, that is God's original message, even if the message of death happens to have been delivered to them first? Is it so much easier, for the original people, to believe the message of death rather than the message of immortality?

If such myths were to be recounted as dreams on the analytic couch, the analyst would, I think, inevitably be led to conclude that the dreamer was expressing through the medium of his dream considerable feelings of conflict, of tension and of ambivalence to death. Undoubtedly some of the myths—or dreams, were they personal dreams—express man's attempt to protect himself against his feeling of complete impotence and helplessness in the face of the inexorable fate of death. He would much rather believe that it is he himself who is—or has been in the past—responsible for the existence of death; for such conviction will help him feel that he is perhaps after all really in control of his life and of his death.

It is of course conceivable that God's intransigence and men's rejection of the second message, the message of immortality, could be understood if one were to assume that we are not really dealing with messages at all, but with spells, with magic, with the power of words. In that case, once the spell is cast, nobody, not even God, can undo it. Yet, on the whole, a belief in spells has, as its complement, a belief in counter-spells; and surely the Great God cannot be thought of as less competent and less well armed with counter-spells than any talented medicine man.

Thus not only the myths in Group III, but also those in Group I, seem to substantiate the hypothesis that man carries inside him not only the need to live and to preserve his life, but also a wish for death. Such an assumption alone can make sense of these contradictory and mystifying stories, which at first sight, like most dreams, appear so inconsequential. As they seem to point in a less disguised form to man's unconscious need for death and extinction, they are perhaps evidence that these needs are less heavily repressed and deflected in the African than they are in the European personality.

As a matter of fact, in these African myths immortality is

conceived of in two different ways. In one case death does actually already exist, together with illness and old age, but it is linked up with rebirth. Such stories tell that men had always been able to rise again like the moon, or to rejuvenate like the snake until that fatal action or accident deprived them of this ability.

But the second group of stories tells of men who lived unchanged and for ever in the closeness to God; here the fatal action terminates the paradisiacal state. In some of these stories work and child-bearing are the dire and unwelcome *consequences* of this rupture with God, this eviction from paradise; in others, however, men start to work and to procreate *in spite of* God's prohibition, and it is this that terminates their closeness to Him. This may well come as a surprise to people in our own culture where the paradisiacal state is always desired and longed for. But some of the African stories describe an almost deliberate attempt to escape from paradise. The Kasai, for instance, tell of a woman who

> cut the navel string that bound together earth and sky, because the closeness of the sky had made men feel unfree.

All such stories seem to describe in dramatic and symbolic form the relation between the systems ego and self, the paradisiacal state or the united world parents representing the self and rebellious man representing the emergent ego.

Perhaps those myths in which a break with God is felt as an achievement appear more readily in those communities in which separateness and differentiation of personality and individualisation are discouraged and suppressed, or else are given only inadequate scope in the social and cultural context; hence the emphasis and value placed on the ego-functions, for they struggle for expression, liberation and recognition. This is in sharp contrast to the situation that faces the European and the American personality, whose need to belong and to feel part of a large and ego-transcend unit is on the whole left unsatisfied.

All the stories with which I have been concerned in this chapter set out to explain how death appeared in the world of man and henceforth became a natural and quite inevitable phenomenon. These stories lack the more macabre and circumstantial quality that marks the explanations and even the rites that accompany the occurrence of an actual death, be it in Africa or in most other societies the world over. For usually such explicit unconscious explanations imply a denial that death is very often ascribed to some aggressive, hostile and destructive wish or act, usually perpetrated in secret by one person against the other, of which the effectiveness is frequently regarded as the result of magic. Or else it is interpreted as the consequence of the revenge taken by some spirit or other for an infringement of some established rule or taboo. And even in our modern and science-orientated world the bereaved relatives seek scape-goats in order to account for a death—the negligence of the nurses, the ignorance of the doctor or the dilly-dallying of the researchers or the indifference of some other relative. As I have described in Chapter 1, however, the reactions to a death and the rituals of death in any particular culture can be very complex, for they often depend on such factors as the age and the character of the person who has died, and on the manner in which he has died.

The co-presence of the origin of death myths on the one hand and of the varied and specific explanations to account for a particular death on the other is indeed puzzling. For the existence of the origin-of-death stories shows that in spite of the apparent preoccupation with explanations in terms of magic, evil spirits, God's punishment or medical negligence, people do, on the whole, recognise death as a natural event. The more overt and frequent occurrence of explanations in terms of malevolence on the part of one source or another, may possibly be due to the fact that such explanations are called for in the case of 'untimely' death—as we saw in the case of the Ibo as described by Noon. And in pre-industrial societies, 'untimely' or 'premature' deaths occur so much more often than death in old age, that is the Ibo's 'death of the gods'. Hence the co-existence of these two apparently contradictory views of death could be understood as a way of saying that although ultimate death is man's inevitable fate, yet death can actually be hurried along, so that it can overtake an 'unnatural' victim. Thus, this sort of answer betrays man's recognition that powerful, if unconscious, anti-life forces exist and do their work from inside man.

The capacity to reach a philosophy of life that involves valuing the existence of death, in spite of the more usual and

75

Dying and Creating: A Search for Meaning

everyday explanations in terms of magic, hostility and rivalry, is really most tellingly expressed by the Kasai of East Africa, when they say:

> Without magic, illness, knives, arrows, war and death life would be just a matter of eating, drinking, sleeping and defecating. Life would be no good without death.

CHAPTER 5

Rites for the dead

A very brief survey of the various death rites the world over may expand further my thoughts regarding man's relationship to death, dying and loss and how he transforms these experiences into potential creation.

Ritualised preoccupation with the dying and the dead seems to have existed ever since paleolithic man. In a recently published book *Western attitudes toward death* (1974), Philippe Ariès suggests that until at least the second part of the Middle Ages, that is until about the thirteenth century, there existed in Western Europe a death ritual, more or less fixed by custom but organised by the dying person himself. Thus, people expected premonitions, signs and signals of their impending death and then they prepared themselves for it. It began with the expression of sorrow at the ending of life, led on to a remembrance of those one had loved and the forgiveness of those who had wronged one. After this one's thoughts turned to God, one prayed for His forgiveness, confessed and then accepted absolution through the priest. After a final prayer the dying person remained in silence, waiting for the end.

Here then a ritual was established for the very act of dying, a ritual which, so Ariès contends, suggests that Western man tended to meet death with a

> sentiment of familiarity with death, with neither fear nor despair, half-way between passive resignation and mystical trust. (p. 103)

Ariès's findings, culled mainly from early and later mediaeval literature, and hence likely to be slanted towards the romantic and the literate, nevertheless underpin the thesis that man's inner world is endowed with archetypally determined drives and phantasies that make death somewhat familiar and, at least partially, acceptable.

Examination of the various death rites that have existed in historic time and survive today produces the impression that it

77

is the purpose of these rites to deal with the personal and the social consequences of death, to give a form, through the ritual, to the emotional experiences and the various stages in the work of mourning, to help both individual and group to stay the threat of disintegration and collapse, and to survive. In other words if the rites are successful, they provide a socially accepted expression for grief and at the same time, by acting as a framework, they help a person to resist the disintegrating force of this grief. Also, by institutionalising signs through which a bereaved person can be recognised by the members of his group, society facilitates patterns of behaviour between the mourner and his group that are relevant and appropriate to his fragile psychological state.

In many cultures death is indeed regarded as a process and death customs may be instituted even before the transition has actually occurred. Thus the dying may be abandoned to their fate or they may be removed to a special place set apart for them. Such a place may then be thought of as specially polluted and dangerous, or else as specially sacred. In either case the place is sensed and reacted to as taboo. For instance, on the Reef Island a sick person is taken to the 'holy house', in order that, so they explain, 'he may die quickly'. Among the Warundi of East Africa the dying used to be taken to a sacred circle, where the priest recited the litany. The Ottoman Jews laid their sick down in a cemetery for 24 hours, with the belief and the intention that they would either die during that period or else make a complete recovery. In most parts of Europe the dying were usually taken out of their beds and laid on the earth or on a heap of straw. A similar custom exists in Malaya. Putting the dying on the earth may arise in part from the need to guard against the pollution of death and from the need to safeguard from the awesome association with death those objects which are not easily replaced, but still needed by the living. But there is also, it seems, a very deep desire to bring the dying into direct touch with the earth, and even the earliest burials seem to have been a symbolic enactment of the rebirth theme, that is of the idea that one plants the body in the earth much like a seed so that it too will germinate there and bring forth new growth in the next season. In parts of India there is the custom of sowing in a hole in the earth the seeds of a variety of herbs, then the charred bones of the cremated person are poured into it and the prayer is chanted: 'Savitri strews thy flesh in the lap of thy mother, the earth' (Savitri being the sun god). This prayer is surely echoed by St Paul when he writes: 'So also is the resurrection of the dead: It is sown a natural body, it is raised a spiritual body.'

Three main reasons for the abandonment and segregation of the dying emerge as the result of the work of students of anthropology and of folklore:

1. There is a widely acknowledged fear that the dying may drag someone loved and alive with him into death.

2. There is the horror and the fear of the corpse; I have already alluded to this in Chapter 1, but a slightly expanded summary may be worthwhile here:

(a) Clearly a corpse creates a sense of confusion and confronts one very directly with the mystery of 'aliveness' and 'deadness'. This person, this 'absent presence' who but a little while ago breathed, reacted, responded and whose appearance is not all that much changed, now lies motionless, inert and totally unavailable. This shocks, puzzles, disorientates and isolates.

(b) The corpse provides irrefutable evidence that all bodies are doomed, sooner or later, to dissolve, to corrupt and to putrefy.

(c) Grief provokes the impulsive temptation to join the dead.

(d) Sometimes guilt is felt that one is still alive when the loved person has fallen victim to death.

3. There is also a widespread fear that the eyes of the dying may fasten on some person who will then be haunted and molested by his ghost. Here I am reminded of Joan, a patient whom I will discuss later in Part II, whose most recent breakdown had been, in part, at least, precipitated by the sight of her dead father. Her family had insisted that she pay him this final visit in the chapel of rest. Although she had been close to him, indeed his favourite child, yet she was haunted several times by him—in dream and in phantasy—in the guise of a malignant ghost. There is of course much fear that the image of the dead person will destroy and replace the image of the living person, perhaps the results of an ambivalence experienced either to the person when he was still alive, or in relation to his death— sadness at loss and anger at loss.

There are, however, also many cultures in which nearness to the dying is sought rather than distance. Among the Greeks, for instance, the nearest relative was entitled to remain close to the dying person so that he could receive his last breath in a kiss. Indeed the last breath is often identified with the soul about to leave its body, its corporeal domain; and if the gifts, talents and achievements of the dying person have been valued and desired, then there is a wish to catch his soul as it escapes. The desire to receive the blessing of the dying is well-attested in the story of Esau and Jacob in the Old Testament, and was a well-established and much described custom in nineteenth-century Europe.

There are a number of interesting rituals that are enacted soon after the occurrence of a death and that seem designed to help the spirit to depart, and in fact to make sure that he does. This might be the reason why in many parts of Europe people open up all the doors and windows of the house in which a person has just died. In some countries people take a tile off the roof, so as to give the spirit a chance to get out. Or they cover over all the mirrors so that the spirit might not be distracted and so lose his way; the custom of carrying the dead out of a house feet first has been interpreted as a method of helping him to find the way out, but prevent him from easily finding his way back. Indeed in many funeral rites special attention is paid to making quite sure the spirit of the dead cannot return—for instance, the route to the burial ground may be particularly tortuous and complicated, rather than the usual direct one; or special openings may be made into the house of the dead, through which he is actually carried out and which are sealed up again and then rendered unnoticeable. Or the corpse may be carried over water or through fire, for these, it is thought, act as insuperable barriers for a ghost. And even the heavy memorial stones, usual in the European world, have the function not only of preserving the memory of the dead, but also of keeping his spirit firmly down in the earth.

Through these various rites men have expressed their very real and strong fear that the dead might return and molest the living or tempt the living to join them. But they are also intended to help the dead acknowledge their new state, find their way about in their new world, find their own place there—and come to rest.

There is also a wish to preserve some link between the living and the dead. This often takes the form of an annual feast or an annual commemoration to which the dead is invited. A special place at the table may be left free for him. In Europe, All Souls' Day has this particular meaning and function and is in fact an important holiday in Roman Catholic countries, together with All Saints' Day which falls one day before it.

In many societies we find grief ritualised in the form of wailing. This may strike the modern Western person as an embarrassing and disagreeable hypocrisy, but its roots lie deep in man's concern that grief, even if excessive, shall be contained in some measured form. Moreover, it is one other expression of man's fears and hopes concerning death and the dead. Thus some peoples have explained that their wailing is intended to drive away the demons who may lie in wait for the soul of the dead. Others hope that it will help the spirit to take cognisance of his new condition and to get used to his new relationship to the people around him, the living. The content of the wailing is usually praise for what the dead person has been, done and achieved in his life, but also a gentle reproach that he has died.

Another very curious but very frequently encountered custom is the Wake. It is of course still practised in Ireland and in the North of England. It is the feasting and carousing of the friends and relatives the night before the funeral. Here too, one of the purposes seems to be to watch over the corpse and to preserve it from prowling demons—or enemies. It is also a watching over the corpse until he recovers from the shock of finding himself dead. Yet it is at the same time a way not only of watching him, but also of entertaining him, feasting with him, reminding him of his past membership of the community and his impending parting from the community. Above all, it is a way through which the individual survivors reassert that they belong to each other, that they are alive and that they must not be and will not be enticed into death.

Indeed the various funeral games, dances and in some cultures even priapic ceremonies, some of which may happen at a stated time after the funeral, all seem to serve the same purpose: the reassertion and reconfirmation of the mourners that they must separate from their dead, bear the loss and resume their functions as persons who are alive.

The need to avoid enticement into death finds expression in

many other details of the death customs. Among the Dyaks of Borneo, for instance, the head of a household calls by name all the children and all the members of the household of the dead person, and they must personally respond to his summons so as to prove that they have really not absconded and secretly followed their dead. A similar intention probably underlies the English custom of 'telling the bees of the death of their owner'. Here the temptation to follow the dead is projected upon the bees, for it is thought that, unless they are told, they too might go away or die.

In many societies the rites carried out on the newly dead are similar to those carried out on the newly born: thus they are usually washed; they may be anointed, that is bathed in oil; put into new clothes or their best clothes; and they may be given a new name.

The way and the place of disposal of the dead can vary considerably, but give some idea of a people's attitude to death and to their dead. In some societies—American Indian, the Parsees of India *et al.*, the bodies are put on platforms or into towers, so that they may desiccate easily and quickly. Some societies use natural or artificial 'caves'—the pyramid is really such an artificial cave—into which the dead are 'sealed'. In many societies the body is buried—in the earth, often quite explicitly conceived as Mother, or the Mother's womb. Such graves may be in some secret place, well away from the habitat of the living; they may be individual and lonely; or they may be communal; or close to the living; indeed in some societies in West Africa the dead are buried inside the houses of the living. This, by the way, often happens to the bodies of children all over the world, for it is hoped that the soul of the child will quickly return to the same parents in the body of a new child. Again, the corpse may be disposed of in water—be it sea or river. Here the reason may be in part the general belief that water is an uncrossable barrier between the living and the dead; but more explicitly, for instance in India and in some of the Buddhist countries like Nepal, the idea of the liquidity of the water and the knowledge that finally all rivers flow together and merge in and with the sea is taken as symbolic of the final fusion and unification of all the souls of all the dead.

The idea of the unification of all the dead is in fact a very general one. In tribal societies this may be limited to the belief in the unification of all 'our' dead, 'our' ancestors. But where tribal religions have evolved towards more universal forms 'our' dead, 'our' ancestors may have become 'the' dead.

This idea of an integration into the community of the dead often underlies the custom of the second burial, which is undertaken at a specified period after the first burial—usually it is forty days, or six months or a year, or even two years later. Such a custom is based on the idea that there is necessarily an intermediate state, when the corruption of the flesh is in process; the flesh is the carrier of all that is personal and unique to an individual, and its putrefaction is felt as terrifying, foul and abhorrent. But when this process has been completed, when the body has been reduced to a kind of anonymity of the bones, the skeleton, then integration into the invisible society is thought to have been accomplished. For now the personal features have been eliminated and the body has become similar to those of the other dead. During the intermediate period, the transitional period, the dead must learn to relinquish the living and the living must learn to re-enter life. When this task has been accomplished, when decomposition has ended, then the deceased really no longer belongs to this world and then his final arrival in the world of the dead is marked by the second burial.

Cremation is also a means of disposal of the dead. Here the idea of the transcendence of separate individuality is usually particularly important. There may be a wish on the part of some nomadic peoples to be able to carry around with them their dead, which is feasible if these are in the form of a small heap of ashes; or there may be the desire to rid oneself, as thoroughly as possible, of a potentially evil and malevolent ghost, be it of 'a witch' as happens in West Africa, or of someone who has died a 'bad' death. But on the whole cremation is conceived as a means of freeing the dead from their bonds to this life and of this, their bodily shell, so that, as the Wayana of French Guinea say, 'their souls may fly up to heaven on the smoke'.

In many societies women are not allowed to participate in the funeral rites, or else they are only given very specific and circumscribed rôles. The reason for this is not far to seek. I have already pointed out in Chapter 4 how men have tended to think—or rather to imagine—that God, holding that procreation and immortality are incompatible, placed before them a choice; and that women, valuing their procreative function above immortality, had led mankind to end up choosing death. Freud, in a little-known but beautiful and important paper, 'The three caskets', describes woman's three basic rôles—he might have said 'archetypal' rôles had he used that particular vocabulary. On the basis of literature and his own clinical work, he concluded that woman is universally perceived as: Mother, sexual partner—and death bringer.

It is, for me, an interesting fact that suicide is almost universally outlawed, and the traditional funeral rites are usually denied to the suicide, as they are to any person who is deemed to be outside the boundaries of the group—children who have not yet been inducted into it, slaves, criminals, and those who have died 'bad' deaths. Such condemnation of suicide is usually explained as a person having robbed his society of one of its members; in other words, he is considered to be a murderer. Indeed, even in English law, suicide was, until quite recently, regarded as an act of felony against the monarch, robbing the monarch of one of his subjects. But the universality of the condemnation of suicide—apart from a few exceptions, when the saving of one's honour is regarded as even more valuable than life—this universality suggests that there must exist a very general temptation to it. Man always tends to react most punitively when someone enacts what he himself has so carefully resisted. And just as the incest taboo would be unnecessary, were there not a general temptation to incest, so the suicide taboo would be unnecessary were there not a general temptation to it.

Much more could be said about the various death rites and they could be discussed in much greater detail. But in this context I may have described them enough to justify the following summary:

1 All transitions are experienced as dangerous, but none more so than the transition from aliveness to deadness.

2 Through the elaboration of ritual a society acknowledges the psychological danger of transitional states. By providing socially acceptable forms, such rituals help the individual to contain and to limit the expression of his emotions without having to deny or repress them.

3. The existence of ritual helps reduce a sense of confusion or disintegration; for it offers the affected person a structured formal expression and it gives him a sense that there is available to him a weight of experience and knowledge that the members of his social group have accumulated and which can then orientate him in terms of his own state, experience and predicament, guide him and reduce his sense of helplessness *and* isolation.

4. Death rituals seem to provide form and expression for the many ambivalent feelings involved when someone one loved— or hated—dies. Thus it seems to provide expression for:

(a) Sadness at the loss.
(b) Guilt—lest one has contributed to occurrence of the death; or perhaps even contrived it.
(c) Guilt that the 'other' is dead while oneself is still alive— there was evidence of such guilt on a vast scale on the part of those who survived the Hiroshima atom bomb.
(d) Anger that the loved person has 'dared' to die and to abandon one.
(e) Dread of, as well as longing for, death for oneself, together with a sharpened awareness of one's own mortality.
(f) Fear—
  (i) that the dead may snatch one from life—a corollary to the experience of dread and longing for death.
  (ii) that members of one's society may accuse one of having brought about the death.
  (iii) that the members of one's group will resent it that one has brought into the group sadness at loss and awareness of the mortality of all.

5. Through the death rites the living can be enabled to feel that they are still connected to their dead and can even be of use to them; for they can help provide them with what they seem to need in their new existence—and this is often conceived in terms of what is known about man's needs in this world— hence the gifts of food, shelter, clothes, shoes, etc. But above all through the rites the living can help the dead to find their way, to orientate themselves in their new world, and they can intercede with the spiritual powers on their behalf so that they will be welcomed and accepted.

6. Finally, the death rites help the mourners to come back to life and to re-integrate into the social community—without excessive guilt and remorse at having apparently separated from and abandoned their dead. In this way their own death wishes are stemmed and counterbalanced. For the various aspects of these death rites seem to imply that the death wish is indeed universal and is aroused quite particularly when death stalks close by.

CHAPTER 6

Psychopathological ways of dealing with death

Once we have acknowledged that death is the most certain event in everybody's life and that, willy-nilly, man carries inside him a knowledge of this fact; once we accept that in order to fulfil his biological destiny man is endowed with a drive towards life and a drive towards death; and once we have conceded that death tends to be used by the unconscious psyche as a symbol for states of fusion, union, and of loss of identity and uniqueness, then many clinical syndromes will acquire a new meaning and significance.

My work with schizophrenic patients in hospital and my work in depth with Clare, whom I have already described in Chapter 2, first helped me to recognise that psychosis can be one way, admittedly an illusory way, of avoiding change and of side-stepping death. For, as I have argued, death tends to be experienced as the loss of the personal, the separate, the ego. Consequently awareness and fear of death must reside in the ego-system and it is this system that death demands as a sacrifice. One way of cheating death is by failing to have an ego available for the sacrifice.

Clare's repeated remonstrances that it was 'all too much' for her—a complaint she made particularly urgently when a new insight, a new area of consciousness was about to emerge and to consolidate—helped me to recognise how much she had invested in remaining unconscious. Every step towards greater consciousness and the consequent strengthening of the ego and its functions, was experienced by her as painful, as an irreversible step in the process of being born. She herself seemed aware of the linkage between death and unconsciousness and of the extremely ambivalent feelings she had about death. 'If only I could stop knowing and thinking, if only I could be unconscious, then I could kill myself and then I would feel no guilt about it.' This was a frequent refrain. Her dreams and phantasies were often filled with images of graveyards and the smell of rotting leaves in late autumn, with houses collapsing and the walls falling in and burying her, with devouring monsters, threatening witches and with crowds that suffocate her. Yet there was also the promise of life and its riches, as for instance in the dream in which a colourless chemical substance is transformed into another one that expands and gives off the most brilliant array of colours.

The psychotic solution to death thus represents an attempt to prevent ego-development and, what is intrinsic to the ego's functioning, awareness of serial time and space. The schizophrenic has sometimes been described as a person who dreams while awake and in terms of the relationship to time and space such a comparison seems appropriate. For just as in dreams, so in the schizophrenic psyche, distance is no object and separateness is not a function of the physical and geographical facts but only refers to the emotional situation; while time has concertinaed, and its march forward has apparently been arrested. I have alluded to this earlier on, in Chapter 1, when I discussed the hero of the fables of immortality.

Of course such psychotic manœuvres fail lamentably; for the arrest of time and space and the relinquishing of the ego-functions (comprising, as they do, awareness of oneself as separate and unique and open to and in touch with the ever-changing world around one—be it social, geographical or seasonal), in order to escape from death and from all ontological anxiety, are actually death in themselves.

I suspect that many 'negative therapeutic reactions' and many resistances to the analytic process have their origin in this fear that with the development of an ego there will also come knowledge of an anxiety concerning the mysterious yet inevitable coming of death.

Another pathological form of dealing with death is the sado-masochistic solution. This has been very well and very interestingly described and discussed by Mary Williams. Here death is dealt with by either identifying with it—which is the sadistic solution—or else by eroticising one's surrender to it. The latter is the solution that Patrick had chosen—though the idea of a choice must not be taken literally, in its everyday sense, since we are of course dealing with deeply unconscious mechanisms and the person himself inevitably feels that such a compulsion is forced upon him, that is it comes, as it were, from outside him. Patrick, as I have described in Chapter 2, was in fact obsessed by his fear of and resentment against death, but in his masturbatory activity torture, pain and death became firmly linked to sexual pleasure and excitement. And indeed in our transference–countertransference relationship his desire to tease me or to hurt me, as well as his attempt to provoke me to attack him, always contained an element of flirtation and sexuality.

An unconscious sadistic solution to death was evolved by Anne. She came into analysis at the age of twenty-three; she seemed to need to cover up her youthful body and arrived for her first session in a loose and colourless overcoat which conveyed the impression of a bent old lady rather than a young girl. Anne spoke in a piping, barely audible voice; she was timid, diffident and solitary. She had been precipitated into an urgent search for an analyst because she felt overwhelmed by terrifyingly sadistic phantasies and compulsions. If alone with one other person she feared she might suddenly thrust a knife either into that person's head or, more likely, into the stomach. She would then be arrested and the following day all the headlines of all the papers would announce her crime, the worst of all possible crimes.

Anne had in fact once brushed up against death when as a small child she nearly drowned in a pond; nor was her early survival assured as she was a twin and both babies were delicate and at risk when born.

The fear of death seemed ever-present; she had little trust in the automatic and efficient functioning of her body and often expressed hypochrondriacal anxiety about cancer, or about choking, because there might not be enough air, or about her heart stopping, unless she constantly and consciously continued to monitor it. She was also afraid that she might impulsively commit suicide one day. And naturally she suffered from severe insomnia and sleep-disturbance.

The murderous compulsion was in marked contrast to the impression she created, with her gentle behaviour and reactions and her more or less conscious fears and apprehensions. Clearly these compulsions were compensatory. For in her murderous phantasies she herself became the omnipotent and implacable enemy, who alone knows when and whom he will strike. Surprise was in fact an important element in Anne's compulsive thoughts. 'There she sits, naïve and innocent; she does not know, but I know that she will be dead very, very shortly'.

Thus Anne's conscious experience of vulnerability and of transitoriness was more than matched by her unconscious identification with the omnipotent and omniscient and undefeatable death, death as reaper and raper.

Paranoia can also be understood as, in part at least, a defensive manœuvre against unconsciousness, fusion and death. Here the ego seems to have acquired sufficient ground in the psyche to encompass a wish to survive and to ward off what is nevertheless experienced as a potentially overwhelming wish for death. But much of this wish for death is experienced in projection, and it is the 'others' who are suspected as potential killers. By creating a world full of enemies, the paranoid person wards off the dangers of love—for loving might bring him too close to his longing and desire for fusion and union. Instead, his suspicions needle him to stay alert, never to let down his guards and to be for ever aware of his own boundaries. All bridges to the 'other' are destroyed; there shall be no intercourse whatsoever. Given this situation and understanding the paranoid reaction as a defence of a poorly established ego against the threat of an excessively strong death wish, it is not surprising that the paranoid person's suspicion should be directed predominantly against the very people who are in an especially close and affectionate relationship to him. If the paranoid delusion acquires a more grandiose quality involving world powers, or even cosmic forces, then such a person probably expresses his feeling that he himself is actually a hero and has to do battle with the dark forces, as heroes always have to do in myths and fairy stories.

Charles demonstrated this mechanism very clearly. He was a young man who was haunted by a sense of isolation, who could not form close and affectionate sexual relationships and whose chief weapon—and guarantee—of his separateness and identity was silence—both inside and outside the analytic setting. He frequently covered his mouth and his nose with his hand in order, as it were, to reinforce his defence against any possible intrusion on my part—though he also expressed dimly veiled hopes that I would penetrate and enter into him. He felt afraid that my thoughts might enter his thoughts and so alienate him from himself. This fear coloured not only his analysis but also his literary work, as he felt himself torn and emotionally undecided as to which of the several heroes he might, could or should identify himself with. Early in the analysis he produced a key image that, I think, graphically expressed not only his own problem but the problem of the schizoid person in general: he saw a round, circular wall made of bricks; but some of the bricks were missing and these empty spaces were liable to tempt 'others' to insert their own there. This bothered him and he resented it strongly. Yet he was also afraid that this wall—and he felt himself, of course to be in the centre of it—would continue to grow and become so high that it would cut him off from all contact with the outside world. And there was the further fear that after all there might be nobody and nothing in the centre.

Charles, like Anne, was quiet, diffident and well-mannered, but his dreams were full of excitement, of violence and death.

At this point I should like to plead that aggression and destructiveness have different roots and different functions and should not be confused. Aggression, as Winnicott also has suggested, is usually in the service of the ego. It is a 'going towards' and aims at the making of boundaries and is resistance to the seduction and the temptation to jettison one's identity. Destructiveness on the other hand issues, as Freud has claimed, from Thanatos and expresses a wish to lessen tensions by reducing the complex to the less complex. Charles and Anne and also Clare really lacked sufficient healthy aggression and were instead driven both in their compulsions and their dreams by destructiveness.

Clearly the obsessional personality is preoccupied with making and re-making order, that is boundaries, because chaos and disorder are experienced as a terrible threat, which like a flood may suddenly break loose, sweep him along and drown him. Furthermore, the 'busy-ness' involved in always keeping order and tidying up might spare him from the experience of empty spaces and silence and thus the risk of encountering his own unacknowledged fears and desires and perhaps the images, the 'pieces of the self' (Gordon, 1963), the archetypal images, emerging from great unconscious depths. The ever-chattering Rudolph, whom I have described in an earlier paper ('The

91

concept of projective identification', *J.A.P.* **10,** 2), comes to mind, for he could tolerate no silence during the analytic hour, made great efforts to control the analyst and the analysis, kept himself feverishly occupied and launched the hypothesis that death is an unnecessary inefficiency, and that all growth can continue for ever so long as the right 'environment' is provided for it. He has since died—of cancer.

Another syndrome—hypochondriasis—is often closely determined by a fear of death. For pain, real or imagined, reinforces awareness that one has a body and that this body and its boundaries can be experienced. After all do we not say, when taken by surprise, that one must pinch oneself so as to know that one is awake? This function of pain to reassert one's identity and to re-assume that nothing unknown to oneself goes on inside oneself was described most unambiguously by a schizophrenic girl, Shirley, when she said to me:

> You can tempt me with food, if you want to tempt me. But really I would rather have indigestible food. And I would much rather have heavy food than soft food. Because soft food dulls the brain. But indigestible food keeps your brain active. Solid food makes one easy and lazy. Take, for instance, pork pie. Now that is indigestible. But then I know that I have eaten it . . . I like to suffer.

Shirley's remarks were echoed for me one day by a patient whose hypochondriacal fears were particularly great and crippling. He started the session by complaining that he could hardly ever remember what had gone on in his analytic session and so he was deprived of 'knowing' all about it. He then told me of a dream he had had the previous night. In this dream there is a cement-mixer and he finds himself eating the cement. This produces discomfort and indigestion and lies heavily inside him. And yet it feels rather good. And he goes on to tell me that after all a good meal makes one sleepy and so one tends to go to sleep and become unconscious. Good food, he muses, gets integrated; one does not really know where it is and what has become of it, and perhaps in the case of a baby a good feed could lead it to confuse the milk-mother with the self, that is with what is experienced as 'I'. If there is pain, such confusion or such surreptitious invasion is avoided.

As regards the manic-depressive illnesses, it seems to me that during the manic phase there is a denial that death is a real and formidable threat. Rather death is treated as something one wants to tease and challenge, to laugh in its face, as an exciting opponent.

But in the depressive phase feelings of loss, of separateness, of isolation and desolation predominate. Depression, it seems, is not so much concerned with the archetypal phantasies of death —that is, with phantasies of dissolution and fusion—but rather with the expected and negative experience of dying.

These few examples may be sufficient to throw light on the relevance to actual clinical work of a study of attitudes to death.

Apart from these major psychopathological conditions I want to end this chapter by pointing to some of the symptoms which, I consider, warrant exploration of a patient's relationship to death.

Clearly, as I have already suggested in Chapter 1, fear of change, of any change, may have its roots in a fear of death; and such fear of change is frequently the basis of a negative therapeutic reaction. Better the pain you know than the pain you don't. Better be dead now than bear the anxiety of not knowing when and how it will happen.

Disturbance in the experience of time may also be related to death. Thus some are over-aware of the passage of time, like the young boy of seventeen who told me that he was obsessed with thoughts of death and terribly aware of the passage of time. As already reported in Chapter 1 he had just realised that he had already lived a quarter of his life. 'I have the odd feeling,' he told me, 'that at one moment I am looking forward to something, say a cross-country run, and shortly afterwards I am looking back on it.' In his case the associations themselves linked death and the experience of the passage of time. But there are also those who live as if time was unlimited, as if they were immortal, and had an eternity in which to accomplish their life-work. Their lives tend always to be provisional and tomorrow is soon enough.

Pathology in the sexual area may also concern relationship to death, in the form of the fear of losing oneself and the terror of surrendering control. Both frigidity in women and impotence in men may express these very apprehensions. The encounter and the interpenetration with the 'other' and the intensity of the psycho-physical excitement of orgasm demand the capacity to relinquish ego controls in the presence of a confidence that such controls will re-emerge and that post-coital separation can be achieved and tolerated.

Certainly the encounter of the death of the 'others' and the whole work of mourning raises the issue of death, mortality and loss. As Landsberg (1953) has so rightly pointed out, the death of the other inevitably evokes awareness of one's own future death and each death may evoke renewed reflections about one's own stand in relation to it and it may force one to re-examine one's conception of life and the value and the meaning of it all. If this task is shunned, then instead of grief there may come neurotic symptoms: depression instead of sadness, feelings of guilt and impotence instead of an acceptance of the rhythm of life and death, and the dead may come to be experienced not as benign presences, but rather as irate, resentful and avenging ghosts. Sleep-disturbances may continue and feelings of imminent doom may linger indefinitely.

Even fear of success and of the resolution of conflicts, to which Plaut has pointed in his paper 'Jung and rebirth' (1977), is relevant to the Eros-Thanatos theme. For conflict and struggle, like physical pain, may be felt as the necessary condition in order to be able to experience oneself as existing, as present. Clearly here lurks an unconscious delusion that paradise, a conflict-free existence, can actually be attained, even in this life.

I do not of course want to suggest that I have here developed a new psychopathology or that I am proposing a sole and universally applicable causal condition. Rather I hope that I have not added but elaborated one other dimension, one other perspective to keep in mind when we explore ourselves or help our patients in their explorations.

To summarise Part I, and the thoughts and hypotheses that seem to have emerged:

1. None of us in this life can know what death is really like; but this does not dispose of the possibility that there may be mental representations of it—whether false or accurate is immaterial.
2. Death seems to be represented in the psyche as a state of non-being, of absorption in a union that precludes separateness and differentiation.
3. Fear of death resides in the ego and is the ego's reaction to the wish for death.

4. Although the need for wholeness and fusion may be over-whelming, compulsive or insufficiently matched by the need for separateness, differentiation and uniqueness, yet it is not in itself necessarily neurotic.
5. Both an avoidance of death and a searching out of death are needs and impulses likely to co-exist in all individuals. In any particular person, however, it might be important and necessary to discover if one of them—and in that case which one—tends to predominate over the other.
6. A good death is one in which there is sufficiently good relationship to self to facilitate surrender—without excessive resentment—to this universal phenomenon, in the presence of a sufficiently well-developed ego, so that a person can die his very own death.

I should like to close this chapter by describing in some detail the relatively short analysis of what I have come to describe to myself as 'the man who remained wrapped inside his dead mother's shroud'.

THE MAN WHO WAS WRAPPED INSIDE HIS MOTHER'S SHROUD

He was the only child of his father's first marriage. His mother had died in childbirth when he was four years old. Then he and his father lived alone together for a while, his mother's sister doing the housekeeping for them. Gradually the situation gelled and father regularised it by marrying his wife's sister, the woman who had kept house for him and his son. He had two more children by this second wife (John's aunt), a girl and then another boy.

John was a builder; his father was a builder; and his uncle, father's brother, was a builder. The three of them worked together as a family business. But there was little doubt in John's mind that his father was the boss, the man with the most intelligence, experience, authority, drive and self-assurance.

John was twenty-eight years old when he came to see me for the first time. He had been referred for treatment because he had become impotent after the birth of his first child. Perhaps it would be better to say that he had lost what little sexual desire and interest he had ever had. He had found sexual intercourse a chore, 'very hard work' and really not as exciting and marvellous as it had been 'cracked up' to be. 'I really could not care less,' he remarked in his flat and unhappy voice. Yet he had sought help! But then it was not only the sexual problem that troubled him. More important and more disturbing did he find his continuing sense of being an inadequate, a weak man; a diffident employer with his staff, a 'wall-flower' at parties, a physical coward in the company of young, strange men, and 'on the edge' of all social relationships.

He had always slept in his parents' bedroom. In his own cot while mother was alive; in father's bed after mother had died; and again in a separate bed when step-mother moved in.

At a first glance he seemed typical of a certain type of middle-class Englishman: he was not dark; he was not fair; he was colourless. He was not small; he was not tall; he was average, a sort of unobtrusive height. He was slim but not thin. He moved as if he took it for granted that nobody would see him. He wore glasses—or did he? He spoke quietly, without any emphasis whatever; his voice was flat, monotonous.

No, he did not feel depressed, he insisted, but I could not but feel his sadness. I guess I had to feel his sadness for him. Until that day when, after several months, he came and told me with a conviction and an animation that had been foreign to him until then, that he had suddenly felt himself emerge out of a fog which had been his world ever since the age of eleven. He was deeply impressed by this sudden awareness of where he had been all this time. 'The fog was at the back of my mind; I somehow knew it was there, but could not get it to come forward. I was so alone in that fog.'

On that day a person, John, was born. His face became more mobile and expressive; and somebody really did come in as he walked through the door into my room. From that day onwards experiences of joy and of sadness, of anger, resentment and of hope opened up to him. The shutters that had been closed, and had kept hidden from him so much of his own childhood, cracked open and slowly he became able to assume the rights and the responsibilities as the lord of his own castle. Much like Sleeping Beauty, he slowly shook off the spell that had cast him into a state of suspended animation. And only then, of course, did he become available to confront the devils and demons who roamed on his estate.

John is the only patient I have had for whom the awakening was so marked and so sudden. But what had happened, what was it all about?

In the very first session John painted for me the backcloth against which I could then see the drama as he was to unfold it before me later on.

It was a scene, chilly, grey, silent, like a wet November day as it drifts over a Norfolk graveyard. There seemed to be nobody there, or if there were they must be as noiseless and as indefinite as figures in a fog. No, he never had been able to 'speak' to his father. He just could not get near him, get 'into' him, any more than he could get 'into' a group of people in the daytime or 'into' his wife at night. Anyway there is really nothing he actually wants or does not want.

Yes, his mother died when he was four years old. But he cannot remember anything about her and he has no image of her. Not till he was nineteen years old did he screw up his courage and ask his father why his mother had died and of what.

In the next few sessions he told me some of his story. One day his mother was taken away. Nothing was said. Then he remembers returning with his father to their empty house; and then somehow he found himself alone downstairs; and there was a noise upstairs, like the miaowing of a cat, and he was petrified. And then somehow he seemed to be at the house of friends; but he is 'screaming his head off'—he cries with despair; he wants so badly, so urgently something, somebody; could it be mother, could it be father? Looking back at it now, might this have been the moment when they buried his mother?

But nobody speaks; nobody explains. Only much later, perhaps a few weeks later, while he is at a bus stop, does a paternal aunt, the sister of his father, tell him that his mother had died.

This is the first and only time that his mother is mentioned.

He remembers visiting his mother's family from time to time. Grandmother is cheerful and pleasant; but even here there is no sign of his mother, no token that she has ever really existed. She is never alluded to and there is not one single photograph of her to be seen.

Nothing is said between him and his father; but he moves from his cot into his father's bed.

And then his mother's sister becomes his step-mother. He

used to call her auntie; he felt no resentment, no conflict, no jealousy; but he continued to call her 'auntie' until he was fourteen years old; after that he stopped calling her anything at all. He felt no anger, no jealousy—he felt nothing.

During the last few years he had become interested in Spiritualism. He now begins to wonder why: was there something he expected from it? Was he already then setting off on the quest for his mother, on a search to find his mother and her son?

After he married he took his wife to his mother's grave in Norfolk. And there he broke down—for the first time and the last time in his life he broke down and he cried. It impressed him, puzzled him.

In these first few months of his analysis John tells his story, quietly, calmly; it is just a story, just an ordinary story, something that happened to somebody. I listen. What a sad little lost boy, I sometimes think. What an elusive emotional coward, I sometimes rage. He talks to me as if to himself. I am there for him, but not perceived by him. He lies inside me. Will I remain the dead body of his mother; the mother to whom one can express one's love only by joining her in death, by creeping back into her womb within which all life and change and striving has come to a stop? Or can we between us summon up enough courage to suffer the son to be hewn out of his mother, to face the unspoken, the unknown; to name it, to shatter the conspiracy of silence, that expedient 'nowhere'?

Of course, life also had found allies inside this boy. Though buried with his mother, a part of him did stay behind and appeased the pain of loss, not by joining the dead mother in her death but by becoming the alive mother in his father's bed. A better and more hopeful attempt to come to terms with his loss, but this also inevitably led to alienation, alienation from himself as a boy, having his own penis and his own potential desire to enter and to penetrate the 'other'. The tug and pull of these contradictions—to be his father's wife and yet subject to his own genital longings expressed itself in his effect on me: at times he seemed so helpless and passive that I felt I ought to have a large penis with which to penetrate him and so create life inside him. And yet it also seemed to me as if, though calling for my active and penetrating penis, yet he could not really offer me an entrance. Instead he maintained the *status quo*—

and so turned back to death, a dead person, unavailable to all, staying dead and hence free from all awareness of desire and so invulnerable to frustration and loss.

At that point he brought his first dream, a fragment of a dream. It is about a sea voyage and a sea captain. He remembers nothing else; but the dream makes him reflect about the sea and all the hazards to which one is exposed at sea—those currents and the submerged rocks. And he shudders. 'No, I would not like the responsibility of piloting a boat. Really that sea captain has nothing to do with me.'

Yet this need to live and to become a person prods him on, ruthlessly; it does not give him his peace. It was a few days after this dream that he came out of the fog.

And then the battles of life began. Awareness of the separateness of himself and mother mentally led him to a growing recognition that in truth she had died. She had abandoned him or else she had been snatched away from him. The sadness at her loss grows and intensifies. He himself now shoulders his sadness. But when he has come to admit to himself that mother has died then, suddenly, the time he had been alone with his father opens itself up to him. And memories of happy moments with father emerge: the games they played, the visits they made, the holidays they enjoyed.

But these good times with his father are wedged between the death of his mother and the arrival of his step-mother. The mystery of death and the mystery of what went on in the parents' bedroom had obviously become confused. One day he ventures to admit how afraid he has always been of water and of the sensation of choking; the terror that someone will hold his head down in the water ... he ruminates, describes; he is anxious and sweats a little. Then suddenly a memory: being in his parents' bedroom and mother coming over to him and putting a cloth over his cot. 'It felt like being held under.'

A few days later he dreams that he gets to the office and finds it all very neat and tidy. He learns that father had decided to retire because he knows that he is ill. The dream makes him feel impotent and envious of a father who seems to know everything and controls everything, even retirement, sickness and death. But he, John, has no idea of what goes on inside himself. He feels sure that one day he will just drop dead and when they open him up they will discover that he had a cancer all the time. Thus although separation from mother had seemed to have happened by now, yet he still carries inside him her lethal pregnancy.

In the course of the next few weeks phantasies of the deadliness of sexual intercourse come to light. The penis is cruel, brutal and dangerous. If he made love to his wife while she was pregnant then he would surely kill her and the baby inside her. Yes, he had felt that father had killed mother in his intercourse with her. Actually he would like to get rid of his own wife. Perhaps if she had another child she too would die in childbirth, and then he and his son could live alone together. He would like to be rid of her. 'Sometimes I think how I could kill her or make her leave me. I could frighten her, she is easily frightened; I think about it quite a lot. I could, for instance, appear like an unexpected but sudden face in the window, like a ghost. She might die of fright. And she is very afraid of snakes. I want her to leave me without me having to feel guilty about it. I would like her to leave me because of my omissions, not my commissions. I should like to starve her out.' For a few days this man who but a few months ago had been so bland and colourless had suddenly become a macabre fellow, capable of making me shudder, capable of forcing me to experience some of the primitive and sinister forces inside us.

But he too, so he then discovers, is in danger, because sexual intercourse is also dangerous for the man; might he not be caught like a fly in a spider's web?

A month after he had lived through these terrifying and destructive sexual phantasies and perhaps because we had succeeded in surviving them, both of us, John resumed sexual relationship with his wife. He mentioned this to me, casually, a few days later. His preoccupations then shifted to the work situation, to his fear of assuming responsibility and to his secret ambitions and omnipotent phantasies. Much of this revolved around his relationship with his father, his envy, his rivalry and then his growing need for independence. He developed ideas about how to expand the business and in fact towards the end of his treatment he started a new subsidiary company. He also developed an interest in the Stock Exchange and found himself fascinated by watching stock grow and expand.

As we met for the last time he remarked that he was pleased to be alive.

Summary and conclusion

The case of John, seen in retrospect, was an uncannily straight-forward one; the phases were clearly demarcated and followed one another in a very direct and almost predictable manner.

It would seem that the struggle between the life and the death forces was unleashed by the boy's inability to bear the loss of the mother, a loss particularly difficult to come to terms with at the age when the genital urges of the Oedipal phase are particularly intense, when sexual phantasies are prominent and florid and when the mother's death is, however dimly this is sensed, caused by the birth of a rival. But, above all, in his particular case the social environment was quite disastrously insupportive and abandoned him in a cruel, if unintentional, way when he most needed help.

Only the psyche's capacity to take refuge in death, in this case in the phantasy of fusion and submergence with the beloved though dead person, enabled John to stay the threat of complete confusion, complete despair or unbearable isolation. Inside the mother's dead body he could in some way carry on in a state of reduced animation, much like an amoeba which, at times of drought, suspends the living processes of nutrition and reproduction by rolling itself into a ball and forming around itself a hard chitinous cyst. There it can rest and let itself be blown about by the wind until it happens to fall once more upon a favourable ground. Then the cyst will burst open and its active life can start again.

PART II

To see a World in a Grain of Sand
And a Heaven in a Wild Flower
Hold Infinity in the palm of your hand
And Eternity in an hour.

William Blake: Auguries of Innocence

CHAPTER 1

Symbols and symbol formation: the crux of meaningful dying and creating

The whole of Part I has been devoted to an exploration of the way in which man has related to the fact of death. This exploration seems to have engendered a growing conviction that creation depends on a continuous interaction of life and death. Reflecting upon my own development as an analyst and on the ebb and flow of my concerns and interests, I have discovered that I myself started out by being fascinated by the expression of the death wish in man; that this has then been followed by a period of preoccupation with the problem of symbols and the health or pathology of the symbolising function; and that shortly after this my attention was caught by the qualities and characteristics of the creative process. I could, of course, try to account for this progression by explaining that these shifts of interest had been determined by the different sorts of problems presented by the different kinds of patients I have worked with during these last few years. Yet my studies of the 'origin of death' myths makes such an explanation seem somewhat spurious; for these stories seemed to demonstrate that men the world over have been aware, even if only semi-consciously, that death and creation are interdependent. In remembering and reflecting upon this I have come to feel that my own development has perhaps after all been strangely reasonable and organic.

By mentioning the 'origin of death stories' at this point I have, I think, done three things: (1) I have tried to understand the development of my own interests in terms of general and universal ideas and reflections; (2) I have recalled the evidence of man's unconscious if not conscious knowledge that death and creation are inextricably intertwined; (3) And thirdly I have drawn attention to the fact that man tends to express his most intimate and most important concerns in and through the language of images and symbols.

Before I immerse myself in a discussion of symbols and the symbolic process, I want to quote a passage from Marion Milner's book *An experiment in leisure* (1939).

> Reason and passion [she wrote] are notoriously utterly unlike—and yet people seem to assume that the transition from one to the other, as a guiding force in living, could be accomplished in a single bound. It seemed obvious to me now, that there must be a mediator between them; then I discovered that Jung had said, of the mythological type of image, that it has the capacity to reconcile idea with feeling, to appear in the rôle of mediator, once again proving its redeeming efficacy, a power it has always possessed in the various religions.

Images, symbols: it is true that through these we relate and we commune with ourselves and with each other, about all that is most meaningful, but also most intangible, to us. They are of the essence of the language of art, of the essence of the language of religion, folklore and dream, and of the essence of the language through which analyst and patient communicate.

And yet, the definitions of the concept 'image' and of the concept 'symbol' are by no means settled or unequivocal. Not only analysts, but also linguists, anthropologists, philosophers, art historians and students of comparative religion have concerned themselves with the concept of the image and the symbol, with their meaning, their definition and their function.

Philosophers have for some time tried to differentiate the symbol from the sign. Philosophers like Susanne Langer, Ernest Cassirer, Roland Barthe, and Louis Arnaud Reid seem to have come to some sort of agreement concerning the sign, which they think of as something to *act upon*, as something 'physical' to which we react directly, in a practical way. Symbols, on the other hand, Cassirer has suggested, are 'charged with meaning' and are infinitely interpretable. And most analysts, of whatever school, would add that symbols always involve affect and feelings.

Leopold Stein, in a paper, 'What is a symbol supposed to be?', tried to get at the meaning of the word by examining its linguistic origins. He pointed out that the word 'symbol' denotes the co-existence of two contradictory actions, of 'gripping' and of 'throwing'. He suggested that it might therefore be translated as a 'throwing together of such things as have something in common'.

Stein reminded his readers that the Greeks used this word in order to refer to 'two halves of corresponding pieces of bone, coin or other object which two strangers or any other two parties broke between them in order to have proof of the identity of the presenter of the other part'. Thus, by presenting his half of the bone or coin, that is to say his 'tally' or his 'symbol', the stranger ceased to be a stranger; for, if the pieces fitted together, it was proof that the two persons had met before and had broken the token into these two matching parts. Thus the link with the familiar and to the known was re-established.

The symbol has frequently been described as a 'bridge'. This is indeed one of its qualities that I consider of primary importance. For the symbol links the strange with the familiar and so forms a bridge between what are really separate objects or experiences. It thus relates the conscious to the unconscious, the here and now to the general and abstract, soma to psyche, physical fact to meaning, the fragment to the whole, and reason to passion.

Freud regarded the symbol as one of the principal defences that the ego employs in its attempt to disguise those unconscious contents—impulses, phantasies or memories—that it experiences as threatening. By offering a substitute for the original but forbidden instinctual goal, the symbol could, so he thought, facilitate the displacement of libidinal urges.

Jung disagreed with what he regarded as a very limited conception of the symbol. He argued that what Freud had described as a symbol was really only a 'sign', because it was merely a substitute, designating no more than the original, the repressed, object.

Jung believed that symbols are in fact the natural language of the unconscious and that they are 'the best possible expression with which to describe a relatively unknown and complex fact, which, though experienced as existing, is not yet fully grasped by consciousness'.

When Jung defines the symbol as the best possible formulation of something relatively 'unknown', I understand him to mean *not* that the symbol describes something that is necessarily 'unknowable', but rather than it expresses facts, relationships and sensuous and emotional experiences that are too complex to be conveyed by mere intellectual formulations.

Arnold Hauser in his *Social history of art* defines the difference between an allegory and a symbol. I found his description of this difference particularly useful because it seemed to be relevant and to clarify the difference between the symbol as conceived by Freud and the symbol as conceived by Jung.

> Allegory [Hauser writes] is nothing but the translation of an abstract idea into the form of a concrete image, whereby the idea continues to a certain extent to be independent of its metaphorical expression and could be expressed in any other form. Compared with the symbol, the allegory always seems like the simple, plain and to some extent superfluous transcription of an idea, which gains nothing by being translated from one sphere to another. The allegory is a kind of riddle, the solution to which is obvious; the allegory is the expression of the static. But the 'symbol' brings the idea and the image into an indivisible unity, so that the transformation of the image also implies the metamorphosis of the idea. In short, the content of a symbol cannot be translated into any other form; on the other hand a symbol can be interpreted in various ways, and this variability of the interpretation, this apparent inexhaustibility of the meaning of the symbol, is its most essential characteristic. The symbol can only be interpreted, it cannot be solved; it is the expression of a dynamic process of thought; it sets ideas in motion and keeps them in motion.

It is clear from all this that image and symbol are closely related; indeed many students of the symbol, particularly art historians, believe that imagery is the essential material out of which symbols are made. Thus Herbert Read describes a symbol as 'an image plus its mental associations'. Cassirer ascribes to the symbol the function of transforming a sense image into a metaphor image; and Susanne Langer suggests that in a metaphor the image of the literal meaning acts as the symbol for the figurative meaning.

An important difference between 'sign' and 'symbol' emerges from this. For a sign need not have a very intimate formal connection with what it signifies. We can have and we can accept certain conventions: the amber light as a traffic signal means 'hold on—something is going to change'—at least, that is what it means in England. Now, there does not seem to be anything essential about amber that could give it this particular meaning. But in symbolism, the form is intimately relevant to the content; the physical configuration itself, the composition, formal patterns, rhythms, colours, shapes, tensions, balances, etc. all carry and are intimately connected with the meaning.

My thoughts about this particular characteristic of the symbol can be clarified further by a study of the concept of art 'as creative aesthetic embodiment', which has been developed by the English philosopher of art, Louis Arnaud Reid. The concept of 'aesthetic embodiment', Reid suggests, implies that sounds, shapes, rhythms, etc. are not only instrumental in conveying aesthetic meaning, but that they themselves help to make and to create the meaning. In other words, what is expressed cannot be grasped apart from the sensuous form that expresses it. Content and medium are indivisible and uniquely united, and the psycho-physical embodiment that is art is a good analogue of our own essentially psycho-physical existence.

Reid himself has explored the inter-connections between his concept of embodiment and Jung's theory of the symbol. Both Reid and Jung believe that the meaning carried by a symbol cannot be expressed in any other way; and both suggest that the symbol potentially mediates the discovery of some new dimensions of being.

It must be clear from what I have already said that I believe the feature that above all distinguishes a symbol from an image, be it in the form of a precept, a sign, an allegory or a metaphor, consists not only in the content but above all in a person's relationship to that content. To take the example of the cross: the cross can be a sign—it can tell us that this man is a Christian monk or that building is a church. But the cross can also function as a symbol: the person kneeling in front of it in a chapel shares, through it, in the birth and life and death of Christ and through his private and personal emotions he participates in the experience of the attitudes and the mythology of the whole body of Christianity.

When one discusses percepts and imagery one really discusses mental contents, the furniture of the mind, as it were. But whether these contents function as symbols or not must depend on the use made of them and on the attitudes adopted towards them. Not all images are symbols; we may delight in their presence and wish for no more. But only when we relate to them as tokens of a different reality, when we 'see a world in a grain of sand' (Blake), only then has the process of making images been transformed into a symbolic experience. In other words, because a symbol interlinks different psychic functions and different levels of experiencing, it has innumerable meanings and can never be totally reduced or 'translated'. A patient brings a dream; but no dream is ever fully analysed. A piece of music is heard, a picture is seen—yet one day one may discover something quite new about it—a new facet, to which one had not been able to respond before. A good example of this is described by Kenneth Clark in his Cosmos Club Award lecture.

> I also remember vividly [he writes] the first moment at which my drawing master at school pulled out of a cupboard some photographs of Piero della Francesca's frescoes at Arezzo . . . Even upside down, as they emerged, I felt a shock of recognition. Some order seemed to have been established, which for the moment set my mind completely at rest. I have been looking at these frescoes, either in photographs or the original, ever since; but when last I left the church of San Francesco in Arezzo, my first thought was that I had never seen them before. I kept on repeating to myself 'How can I have been so blind?'
>
> Well, that has been, and is increasingly, my experience before all great works of art, and I suppose it is the same with everyone who responds to them.

Indeed this can also be experienced by analyst and analysand as they return again and again to the same dream, the same phantasy—but with some new insight and with some new understanding. For, where a symbol operates, there is always meaning-behind-meaning-behind-meaning.

In the beginning, analysts were above all concerned and interested in the content of a symbol; they were fascinated by what so-and-so *really* meant. Did a church tower symbolise a phallus, the dog something that fights or bites, or the fighting instinct? They were thus quite absorbed with what one might call the job of transcribing or translating the symbol. And even Jung, so Louis Reid suspects, did seem to hanker after the translation of symbols into conceptual terms.

As early as 1916, however, in his paper on 'The transcendent function', Jung had shifted in his definition and description of the symbol from the study of the *content* to the study of the *process*. In that essay he referred to the 'symbolic attitude', which he characterised as having an 'as if' quality built into it. But the notion of symbolic attitude refers to the relationship of an ego to an inner psychic content. Indeed Jung claimed in that essay that whether any particular mental content—be it image or thought—functions like a symbol depends essentially upon the presence of this 'symbolic attitude'; in other words, upon the quality of the approach brought to this content by the ego.

It is this capacity of the mind to form symbols, not only in terms of content, but above all in terms of their function, that Jung has called the 'transcendent function'. Jung describes the transcendent function as developing from the interaction of conscious and unconscious contents, thus making for easy transitions from one attitude to another: unconscious contents must be supplemented by conscious attitudes.

He claimed that it was the rôle of the analyst to mediate the transcendent or symbolic function for the patient. The analyst does this by remaining aware of both the conscious and the unconscious themes, wishes, phantasies, communications and transactions, and by tolerating the tensions resulting from the often contradictory feelings that the patient experiences—love, hate, anger, seeking, withdrawing, etc. He may have to carry the projections of internalised personages or conflicting wishes until the patient's ego has developed sufficient strength to re-integrate the projected bits.

Jung had called this symbolising process 'transcendent', not because he wanted to ascribe to it a metaphysical quality, but because he thought of it as a function that creates transitions from one attitude to another and so helps a person to transcend an existing and familiar state of experience or stage of development.

If the transcendent function fails to be activated then a 'symbolic' *content* might very well remain quite ineffectual in terms of stimulating the growth and development of a person. In fact without the 'as if' attitude a symbolic content may either be acted out in a delusionary manner, or else it may lie around like deadwood, like an *objet d'art* in a collector's glass case. There are indeed many patients who produce powerful symbolic material, but who do not use it symbolically.

To give an example: a patient, a middle-aged, rather formidable-looking woman, produced plentiful material concerning the terrible Great Mother—in her associations, in her dreams, in her perception of the people around her, in her relationships to them—and, in the course of analysis, in her relationship to me. But she was really identified with the Great Mother and acted it out in relation to her daughter. Her failure to develop a symbolic attitude had almost proved fatal for the development of the adolescent girl. The latter had obediently regressed to the state of a helpless baby in response to her mother's wish to have her at home, if necessary sick and in bed, rather than tolerate the separation of letting her go out of her sight—to school. Only when, as a result of analysis, a de-identification with this archetypal image had occurred, could the patient herself begin to develop, could a person emerge with an individual identity; only then could she begin to tolerate some change, some growth, some separateness, acknowledge the different needs of different persons, and become aware that children at different stages of their development need a different type of mothering. Then could she also begin to relate herself to the helpless and hurt and frightened child inside her. This then broke up, at last, the matriarchal pattern that had gripped her family for at least three generations.

The capacity to symbolise, that is the capacity to experience, simultaneously, the known and the unknown, the 'I' and the 'Not-I', physical experience and spiritual experience, this capacity has a history, a developmental pattern, which can be either furthered or obstructed. In Part I, Chapter 2, I summarised very briefly those stages in psychological development that I considered to be particularly relevant to a study of the developing personal stance both towards death and towards creation. I described there the stage of the *original self*, when there is as yet little differentiation and little experience of boundaries, a stage marked by 'oceanic' feelings and the experience of 'participation mystique'. I then went on to describe how, as a result of a growing need for independence, separateness and uniqueness, the process of 'deintegration' (Fordham's concept) or differentiation accelerates; this then helps the individual to recognise himself more and more easily as a separate entity which, if all goes well, he can now experience without feeling too much panic or discomfort. But only when the major psychic systems, the self, the ego and the shadow, have been established and consolidated can the symbolic, that is the transcendent function, with its 'as if' attitude, emerge and develop.

The emergence of the symbolic function can then be taken as a sign that considerable psychic differentiation has occurred, that there is now in the individual enough separateness between himself and the world—both outside him and inside him—for a bridging process to be feasible, necessary and valid. In other words the stage has been reached when the individual wants to and can attempt to re-relate to one another his needs for the personal and unique on the one hand and his needs for containment, togetherness and union on the other; needs for objects and facts, and needs for meaning and significance.

The symbolic function has, so I believe, the following antecedents.

Its most primitive ancestors are sensations, sensory experiences and the archetypal images. These archetypal images seem to be in many ways analogous to what the ethologists have described as 'innate release mechanisms'; that is to say they are the mental configurations that help release instinctual behaviour in the presence of the appropriate stimulus. Jung has also described them as portraits of the instinctual goals. I have recently heard a physician, in his attempt to come to grips with this concept, call them 'programmers'.

The next and nearer ancestor of the symbolic function is what Hannah Segal has described as 'symbolic equation'. By this she meant the experience of two separate objects being are thought of in such a way that the existence and the characteristics of one of them is denied, because it has in fact been totally assimilated and absorbed in the other. Segal gives as an example the case of a schizophrenic patient, who had so completely equated the violin with the penis that he could not in fact play his violin in public. In other words, the violin had ceased to exist for this patient as a separate entity, with its own sensuous and individual characteristics; he had eliminated it.

The symbolic or transcendent function is then the third stage in man's attempt to bring order into his perceptions, to familiarise himself with the world and with himself, to increase his understanding and so imbue with meaning the world and his experience of it. The symbolic function, because of its 'as if' attitude, involves the experience of representation instead of identification, and the recognition of similarities in objects that are, at the same time, known and acknowledged to have a separate existence.

I must, however, emphasise here that I do not believe that a person uses always only one of these three stages of the symbolic function. On the contrary: I expect a good deal of variation and inconsistency. Mental contents that carry little or no emotional conflict are likely, in adults at least, to be readily available for symbolic expression; while conflict-ridden and highly affective contents may be expressible only in terms of symbolic equation, or even, as in the case of the patient I have just described, they may be expressed in primitive, archaic and archetypal image forms. Yet, if an individual relied entirely on symbolisation his experience, his life, might actually become impoverished. In artistic work and creation, for instance, symbolic equation is likely to play an important—even if transitory—part. The actor who has sunk all awareness of his own identity into the part he is to play, the painter absorbed in the object that has triggered off his fascination, the musician engrossed in the sounds that fill his inner ear, all these are probably at that moment nearer to symbolic equivalence than to symbolisation, and as a consequence their work acquires a quite special flavour of conviction and emotional intensity.

The material from two patients may, however, help to show how the capacity to symbolise can be crippled and seriously impaired if certain developmental conditions have not been fulfilled; and how, in particular, the problems of death, of mourning and of separation anxiety can ravage the transcendent function.

The two patients I have in mind are Joan, an English woman in her middle thirties, and Rudolph, a man of German origin, in his early forties.

Joan was asthmatic and suffered from severe insomnia. She was compulsively indecisive, and prone to enact various self-protective rituals, such as covering all mirrors and removing all objects like stockings or belts with which she feared she might be strangled. These rituals took place at night, before going to bed. Ever since adolescence she had had periodic breakdowns, which had been characterised by moods of anxiety and depression, though expressed in a rather histrionic manner.

Rudolph experienced somatic sensations—usually of the growth or shrinkage or change of various parts of his body. These were actually delusional in quality. His relationships to people were marred by his temptation to act out both his omnipotent and his paranoid phantasies.

Both patients were greatly troubled by death. Both had lost their fathers, Joan while she was in her early twenties, Rudolph when he was only seven years old. Neither of them had been able to complete the work of mourning. Rudolph was haunted by dreams of his father's coffin, which was sometimes safely closed, but would at other times open up to reveal or to spill out the gruesome remains of what had been his father. Joan tended to be pursued or confronted by her father's malignant ghost. Thus she had one dream in which she was alone in her house; someone knocked on the door—she opened it and found there her father's ghost looking evil and threatening and demanding that she come away with him—back into the world of the dead. Another time she brought a hypnogogic dream; she was with me in the consulting-room. Her father lay on the couch. When she would not lie with him, I went to lie on top of him; and when I refused to move she attacked us—me and her father—with a sword. Thus both analysands were in the grip of their dead, with whom their own identity was much confused. Joan was the only one of her siblings to suffer from all the psychosomatic symptoms of her father; nor could she conceive for herself a destiny that might be different from his. Rudolph expressed his identity-confusion in terms of the coffin: sometimes he recognised it as his father's; sometimes it was his own.

Joan tried to defend herself against the fear of death by denial. This took the form on the one hand of 'flirting' with suicide; on the other of escape into an illusory alertness, a compensation for her compulsive indecisiveness. Rudolph sought his defence against the fear of death by clinging stubbornly to the belief in the immortality of the body. I have already alluded to him in Part I, Chapter 6.

Both patients showed a ruthless greed for their analyst. They both experienced the ending of each session as catastrophic and devastating. The experience of their separateness seemed to be felt by them as a tragedy; they tried to undo this by an unceasing effort to fuse with me, and by attempts to control me and to manipulate me, as if I were a part of their own body or they a piece of mine. In other words, both experienced acute separation-anxiety, from which they tried to escape by omnipotent manœuvres.

The analytic material of both patients showed a great deal of preoccupation with eating and with food.

It was characteristic of both patients that they seemed to want to protect themselves, each in their own way, stubbornly and almost with panic, against any growth of insight, awareness and real consciousness.

In the case of Joan the capacity to experience symbols was so undeveloped that even dreams, images and phantasies were at first very rare and very meagre. She seemed able to respond only to what was concretely and tangibly present. Rudolph, on the other hand, produced a welter of images, associations, phantasies and delusions. But he tried to abort any development of the symbolic function by idealising 'the unconscious'. Jung has in fact drawn attention to the danger of what he has called the 'aesthetic tendency', that is the tendency to overvalue the formal worth of the phantasy products of the unconscious, which then diverts the libido from the real goal of the transcendent function. I think Marion Milner describes just this in her *Experiment in leisure* when she writes about

> the turning inwards blindly, which is actually a retreat from the reality of fact, rather than a way of reaching it. Clearly it was the confusion between these two ways of turning inwards, the blind grasping after dream pleasures, and the seeming willingness to let all pleasure go and simply wait ... For I had certainly spent much of my life in fruitless running after the coloured parrot's feathers of fancy, fruitless because it was blind, it was imagination still in the service of desire rather than of fact.

Rudolph acted out this particular defensive escape into the 'aesthetic tendency' either by demanding that I *ask* his unconscious what *it* was thinking—which he tended to do whenever I had given an interpretation through which I had hoped to create some awareness and forge some lines of communication between his incipient ego and his unconscious phantasies. Or else—which was a more common state of affairs—he would juggle so fast and furiously with the many images and phantasies he experienced, that their symbolic linkages were continuously un-made, re-broken, re-muddled and re-confused.

Consequently analytic sessions were often orgies of so-called 'free association'. He would stay with an image a short time only, and take flight as soon as the danger of having to bear its affective impact became too imminent. He often made me feel that we were enacting a sort of treasure-hunt, for he seemed to be dropping bits of clues as he fled from one hiding place to another.

The impairment of the transcendent function in these two patients, was, I would suggest, closely bound up with their attraction to and their fear of death; with their intolerance of separation and separateness; and with their ruthless greed.

These three characteristics seem to me to be symptomatic of an overwhelming need to preserve the original self, the original state of fusion. They were, I think, in the case of my two patients, symptomatic of the fact that the need for fusion far out-balanced their ego needs for consciousness and differentiation.

To elaborate on the way in which I think about each of these three syndromes:

I have recently come to believe that greed is really another manifestation of an unconscious resistance to the process of separation and differentiation. In fact it seems to me to be a reaction of panic to any growing awareness of one's separate-ness. For it is probably the body's metabolic functions that give the baby one of his first experiences of separateness, of change, and of temporality. And it is very likely that it is the recurrence of hunger pains that informs him that what he eats, and so incorporates, does not in fact become his own, or himself, once and for all. The experience of defecation proves to him further that he cannot hold on for ever to what is inside him. Thus he gains an awareness—however dim and vague this is bound to be—that all is in constant change, and that even his own psychosomatic existence is anything but stable and per-manent. Greed, in this context, might then be seen as a desper-ate attempt to avoid the possibility of ever having to experience hunger; for hunger is a sign that one is, inescapably, separate, and subject to change and to time. Through greed a person seems to express the hope—however vain and doomed to failure—that he can escape all experience of hunger and so feel forever in a cosy state of unconsciousness.

The wish to feel oneself as an unchanging and self-sufficient system, expressed perhaps in myths in which a god—Prajapati, a Vedic god of India, for instance—eats what he creates, is probably at the root of some psychosomatic symptoms like constipation or asthma. Joan was in fact asthmatic. Through such symptoms a patient may reveal and express his wish that time stand still and all change stop.

Intolerance of separation is, of course, most severely taxed when someone whom one has loved, cared for or depended on, dies. Bowlby has written much about the problem of the mourn-ing process. He has shown—and my own clinical experience has certainly confirmed this—that if there is excessive resistance to separation, and if a person relies on denial as a defence against the pain caused by the death of another person (or if, in the case of a child—as happened to John, whose case I have already described—the family and the whole environment conspires to deny a death) then the relationship to the dead person is not available to the symbolic process, through which alone a new attitude, a new relationship to the dead person can become possible. In the case of Joan and Rudolph, their strongly ambivalent relationship to their fathers, while these were still alive, had probably increased their difficulty in completing the work of mourning.

Psychoanalysts have suggested that mourning cannot be completed unless the individual is endowed with enough capacity for 'reparation'. As an analytical psychologist I find the concept of reparation not quite sufficient; I would want to amplify it and say that in order to accomplish the mourning process, the deep, archetypal themes of death, rebirth and transformation need to be activated.

This brings me to the third syndrome, which I believe hinders the development of the symbolic function, that is the inordinate attraction and/or the inordinate fear of death. I have already said a great deal about it. But in the case of the two patients I am discussing here, the theme of death and the strongly ambivalent feelings experienced about it, were quite explicit and unmistakably voiced and communicated in the course of the analytic work. They made it quite clear that the death of the parent was felt, in some ways, as their own death, and that the precarious balance inside them between the life and the death wishes had in fact been severely shaken by that death. When I think about these two patients, and in particular of the dreams they brought—the dream of the coffin or the dream of the father's angry, malignant and threatening ghost, I am reminded of the custom among the Dyaks of Borneo, which I have described in Part I, Chapter 5, where at the time of a death the head of the family calls every member of his kin by their name and demands that they assemble before him.

Returning to the psychological roots of the symbolic function in the individual, I must briefly make mention of Winnicott's contribution to the understanding of it. In his paper 'The location of cultural experience' (Winnicott, 1971) he proposed the concept of the 'transitional object' and he showed there that such a concept could have wider implications in that it

could come to act for us as a bridge connecting our understanding of the inner world of phantasy to the outer world of
culture. Winnicott named as a 'transitional object' that teddy-
bear, or blanket, or sucking vest or whatever, to which an
infant becomes deeply attached, which he tends to hang on to
during the day and usually takes to bed with him at night. This
object the infant claims to possess. Winnicott has suggested that
the 'transitional object' is something that is both given to the
child and created by the child. It represents, it incarnates, his
first attempt to reconcile reality and phantasy, inner world and
outer world. It is thus the earliest expression of man's creative
drive, of his symbolising capacity and of his concern with
meaning, which can later become verbalised as 'What is life all
about?'. The importance of the transitional object lies not in its
symbolic value alone, or in its actuality alone, but in the fact
that it carries the potentially positive quality of a paradox. On
this attempt at reconciling reality and phantasy, Winnicott has
proposed, is then built the foundation of what he has called the
'third area' or 'the area of experience'; this becomes the source
of play, of imagination, of culture, religion and art. And what
Jung has described as 'psychic reality' can be defined as the
essential content of the area of experience.

Profiting from his imaginative linking of man's most sophisticated pursuits with one of his earliest ones, Winnicott has then
made some incisive comments about culture itself. He suggested,
for instance, that culture is the result of the interplay between
originality and inventiveness on the one hand, and of the
acceptance of tradition on the other. It represents therefore a
creative integration of man's need for fusion and the experience
of belonging—in other words, expressions of the death wish
centred on the self—and his need for separateness and uniqueness—that is the life wish, centred on the ego. Extrapolating
from this model, he then suggested that the plagiarist, for
example, is someone who cannot relinquish the state of fusion
and identification; and so he walks around in other people's
clothes, despairing that he will ever be able to have, or to make,
his own. On the other hand the person, or the artist, who
isolates himself and denies the relevance and the value of all
tradition is really also in a state of fusion and identification; but
in his case it is identification with an archetypal image, like
the Great Mother, or God Himself. This prevents him from

emerging out of the state of primitive omnipotence. Thus neither have come to terms with the reality either of the external world, or of their own personal existence. Both rebel against mortality, the former by denying or hiding his personal existence; the latter by identifying with the Immortal.

The value of Winnicott's formulation of the 'area of experience' lies in the fact that we can now locate that psychic area where sensuous experience meets imaginative invention, where cognitive activities are brought into relationship with emotional activities and where the need for order and meaning finds expression in the creation or discovery of forms that embody experience. He also makes clear why playing is such an important forerunner of creative work when he points out the link between the emergence of play activity and the development of the area of experience, and when he reminds us that playing consists in the 'manipulation of external phenomena in the service of the dream'.

In my work with patients I am left in no doubt that a person who cannot play, whose perfectionism, obsessional defences, or fear of criticism do not allow him to play, is banned from the joys of making and creating and is crippled in his capacity to feel truly alive.

The importance and seriousness of playing has for some time tended to be under-emphasised. Yet as early as 1931 Jung wrote that

> the creative activity of imagination frees man from his bondage to the 'nothing but' and raises him to the status of one who plays. As Schiller says, man is completely human only when he is at play.

Winnicott has added to our understanding of man's need for meaning and for self-transcendence by discovering some of the experiential roots and early forms through which these needs and tendencies first make themselves manifest.

CHAPTER 2

Reflections on clinical technique resulting from a review of the nature of symbolisation

If we really think that the symbolic function has crucial importance—that in its absence men can exist, but cannot live —and if we assume that the life and death forces—activity and passivity, ego and self—are intimately interwoven in the symbolising process, then this cannot but express itself in our work as analysts. For this is likely to affect the goals we have in mind for our patients as well as the function and rôle we see as our own.

It is this kind of attitude and approach that, I believe, informed in large part the development of Jung's technique. It led him, for instance, to a feeling of dissatisfaction if the analyst relied solely on reductive analysis. And indeed to be *exclusively* concerned with the discovery of causes and determinants is likely to leave a patient with a rather sterile and barren inner world, in which only reparation rather than creation is conceivable, and in which, as a matter of fact, even sensations and a sensuous relationship to the world are actually undervalued and sacrificed on the altar of ideation. After all, does he not live in a poor world who thinks that the pleasure he experiences when climbing rocks, entering caves or walking through forests is really just a substitute for the unconsciously experienced pleasure he takes in the contact and exploration of his mother's body? Such 'knowledge' could alienate him from the reality of his actual sensations, in the here and now. It could cut him off from the smells, the touch, the sounds, the forms, the colours and all the other things that happen on mountains, in caves, and in forests—and, by the way, also from the actual experience, now as well as then, of his real mother, who, to the infant, must be a complex pattern of smell and touch and sight and sound, provoking experiences in many parts of his body.

Indeed, exclusive use of reductive analysis might provoke, support or maintain the stage of symbolic equation, when the identity of one object is absorbed into the identity of another.

The apprehensions he felt about the exclusive use of reductive analysis, and the value he placed on the symbolic process and man's very basic need to create, led Jung to experiment with what he called 'active imagination'. He thought of it as a technique that might be helpful to people who had had, or were nearing the end of their personal analysis. Active imagination could thus become a technique of an, as it were, internalised analysis so that the ego takes over the functions of the observing and receptive analyst in the presence of freely flowing images and phantasies, or the actual creation of pictures or sculptures or musical or verbal forms and patterns. I think he would have regarded Marion Milner's *On not being able to paint* as well as her *Experiment in leisure* as products of a successfully conducted active imagination.

When, however, one discusses 'active imagination', one needs to keep firmly in mind two kinds of reservations: for such a do-it-yourself analysis can provoke a lot of rash and over-optimistic enthusiasm. In fact real and serious active imagination is an arduous, slow and at times painful process, which has many pitfalls. Jung himself has warned against two of them. One is the danger of the aesthetic tendency, to which I have already referred when I discussed Rudolph's defensive idealisations. The other is the opposite danger, the danger of being in a hurry to 'understand'; to make sense of, to push the emergent contents from the unconscious into a 'form'. Jung thought this latter danger to be due to an over-valuation of *content* as opposed to *experience*. I think of it more as a flight from the tension and terror of the uncertain, the unknown. A similar recognition of this particular danger has been expressed by both Marion Milner and also by Anna Freud in her foreword to Milner's *On not being able to paint*. They compare there the beginner painter with the beginner analysand and point to the dangers of their 'unwillingness to accept chaos as a temporary stage', to their fear of 'plunging into non-differentiation', to their disbelief in the 'spontaneous ordering forces' and hence to the attitude of haste and anxiety that can lead painter, analyst, analysand—or any other person at the cross-roads of something new—to premature interpretation; for these would then close the road and stop the spontaneous upsurge of unconscious material.

Something similar seems to happen and to explain certain group phenomena, as I have observed them in work with groups. Thus when individuals find themselves thrust together into a group—particularly a large group—not knowing each other, not understanding the tensions produced, feeling their personal identity threatened, all these discomforts seem to provoke the making of facile and yet potentially dangerous group constellations: the making of leaders, of scapegoats, the expression of paranoid ideas and the hopes of magical salvation. For uncomfortable knowledge does seem preferable to no knowledge. Yet fear of regression to an undifferentiated state leads to a negative attitude towards creativeness. It is because of these dangers that Jung believed that, although active imagination is a method through which conscious and unconscious experiences can be brought face to face, so that an effective interchange can take place between them, yet it is a method that can only be used by 'carefully selected cases'; for it could carry the patient too far away from reality, unless he has developed a relatively strong ego.

Michael Fordham has made the, to me, valid distinction between 'active imagination'—that is, imagination which goes on while a person, who has enough ego to serve as observer, is alone—and 'imaginative activity' by which he means imagination that is more primitive and undirected by any conscious purpose. Probably most of us are really indulging in 'imaginative activity' when we hopefully think that we are doing 'active imagination'. Marion Milner seems to have caught herself out at that, as she confessed in the passage in her book *An experiment in leisure*, where she described herself as 'running after the coloured parrot's feathers of fancy'.

For a time the technique of 'active imagination' seemed to have been relegated to the background of our thinking in England. It seemed too difficult and too hazardous, and perhaps too irrelevant to analysts having to deal with very ill patients and also with child patients. In 1966, however, Dorothy Davidson rescued this concept by suggesting that the transference–countertransference relationship between patient and analyst is often an enactment, in the here and now, of the unconscious drama in which the patient has been held prisoner, and that such an analysis can be viewed as a form of 'lived-through active imagination'. In other words, while Jung thought of active imagination as an *intro*-personal enactment of a drama, Davidson suggests that active imagination can also happen *inter*-personally, in the transference.

What is interesting in this recent extension of the concept of active imagination is that such use and understanding of active imagination can happen only when the analyst also is prepared, as he expects his patient to be prepared, to expose himself to all the anxiety and un-ease that symbolic and creative experience can bring. In other words, for such inter-personal 'active imagination' to occur the analyst must himself be able to take the risk of regressing to a less differentiated state—though it be controlled by his own watchful and observing self.

When concern moved from the analysis of symbolic content to a concern with symbolic process then analysts re-discovered that their own affective responsiveness needs to be available to the patient as well as their intellectual responsiveness. This could mean that at times the analyst has to accept his patient's need to fuse with him, and he must come to understand that this is in fact an essential and recurrent phase in the development of all creative relationships. Accepting this and, when the time is ready, being seen to accept it, may sooner or later encourage a patient to expose himself also to these risks in relationship to himself and to his inner world. And thus he too may be progressively more ready to become that empty vessel that from time to time one needs to be, if one wishes 'to be filled', as Lao-Tze has taught.

Through an increased understanding of the nature and the function of the symbolic process and the use analysts have learned to make of it in their clinical practice we have discovered, I believe, those psychological processes that help an individual to span the gap between his personal and his collective history. And if Winnicott is correct then indeed the contents of the 'third area' are neither purely inner nor purely outer, neither purely factual nor purely imagined, neither purely private nor purely public. Thus when a symbol functions truly symbolically, it links the past to the present, the private and unique to the social and cultural, and archetypal processes to ego processes; and thus it becomes a bridge between the forces in the service of ego-making and the forces in the service of ego-transcendence. And through the symbol, history—both personal and collective —is transformed into relevant and experienced actuality, private emotions and phantasies become shareable forms of communication, personal experience can *expand* into collective experience, and collective experience can *condense* into personal experience.

As a consequence of this more comprehensive conception of the symbolic process, the analyst must nowadays try to be in a sensitive rapport with his patient's past as well with his patient's actual situation and actual emotional experiences, and with the formal qualities of his communications as well as with their content. He can thus mediate for his patient an ever-growing ability for symbolic experience, which involves the emergence of ever new forms of synthesis of the opposing psychic forces and attitudes; and thus the confrontation of the wishes for death and fusion and the wishes for identity and uniqueness may lead to the emergence of new, genuine and creative work, life styles and personal growth.

PART III

What we call the beginning is often the end
And to make an end is to make a beginning.

T. S. Eliot: Little Gidding

CHAPTER 1

The nature of the creative process

I was attracted to Jung's theories by the seriousness with which he treated man's need to create and the importance he gave to this need. As early as 1929 Jung had actually classified creativity as one of the five main instincts characteristic of man, the other four being hunger, sexuality, the drive to activity and reflection.

What then is creativity? What might be its nature and quality? Before I go any further I want to make it quite clear that it is my belief that the process of creation will always retain an element of mystery; and I doubt that we shall ever fully penetrate into it. But we may gain more understanding of those conditions and circumstances—external and internal, personal and social—in which the mystery of creation can and may happen.

In recent years creativity has often been defined or understood in terms of inventiveness, productivity, originality or novelty, while criteria like meaningfulness, value or excellence have tended to be glossed over. Though creativity has indeed something to do with all these qualities, yet it is none of these alone.

Those who have recently tried to construct creativity tests have really been misled, and they mislead, for such tests tend to neglect considerations of relevance and quality, and concern themselves instead only with quantity or with fluency of association. These qualities may well be worth investigating, but it is false and presumptuous to imply that such information is relevant to or is even identical with 'creativity'.

Nor is it justified to identify the 'creative' with the 'artistic', for creativity can function in relation to many different activities, including the sciences, technology, a person's relationship to others—human, animal and inanimate—as well as in his relationship to himself and in particular to his own growth and development. Thus it is important to keep in mind the difference between (a) the creative process, and (b) the product of the creative process. It is true that artists, probably more than anyone else, have been interested and concerned with the actual process and the actual experience of the process of creation and have thus provided many insights; furthermore, making 'art' involves perhaps a particularly large number of different mental activities such as making, forming, inventing, discovering, learning, experimenting, feeling, thinking and doing. Consequently much of the little we know about the nature of the creative process we owe to the self-examination and introspective work of artists.

Essential to and underlying the creative process is the search for meaning; and meaning, so it seems to me, evolves out of a synthesis of the process of differentiation and ordering on the one hand and the making and discovering of something new on the other. It is thus inseparable from the capacity for awe and wonder and from the courage to be genuinely available to any kind of experience, however unfamiliar, new, bewildering or unknowable it may be.

Engagement in a creative process depends, I believe, on a person's capacity to mobilise contradictory but mutually reciprocal qualities: activity and passivity; consciousness and unconsciousness; masculinity and femininity; receptivity and productivity. The interaction and interdependence of these contradictory qualities emerge clearly when one looks at the stages of the creative process as these have been discovered and identified by researchers, artists and scientists. Nearly all of them seem to agree that there are four of them; but their relative importance or their relative duration may vary from one person to another, from one activity or discipline to another, or even from one particular creative act to another in the same person. What is more, the process may be a continuing one, so that the last stage in one work or one part of a work can lead on to the first stage in the next phase of a work, or to an altogether new work. In other words, these four stages have to be recognised as elastic and merely as schematic descriptions of the process of creation.

These four stages are:

(a) A *preparatory* stage, when a person immerses himself in a problem and feels himself drawn into a period of conscious concern and struggle. Here conscious ego control and the differentiating functions predominate; knowledge and relevant skills are acquired; the problem poses itself and challenges to battle. In order to enter this stage and keep faith with it, a person needs to be humble but persistent. For unless he is humble he cannot acknowledge ignorance and doubt, and if he does not acknowledge them he cannot learn. Yet he must not be overawed by his ignorance, for this could prove too discouraging and so weaken the persistence he needs for learning.

(b) In the second stage, the stage of *incubation*, a person 'sleeps on the problem' either literally or metaphorically. It is the stage that the philosopher Whitehead has described as an experience of 'muddled suspense'. At this point one feels one has run up against a wall; so one lets go of it, withdraws one's attention from it, takes one's mind off it. Instead one now feels baffled and confused. It is at this stage that doubt and pain and anxiety and despair rack and torture him who would create. Should he flinch, seek refuge or attempt a short-cut, he will either return to that which has already been and so enter upon the process of repetition, stagnation, putrefaction or petrification. In that case what he then produces will turn out to be banal, stereotyped or slick. Or he will lose his roots altogether, inflate and, like a balloon, drift off into the air. It is during this stage of incubation that a seed may take root—but if it does, it happens unseen, in the depths of the unconscious psyche, in the dark. And then, *if* he is lucky, the third stage may 'happen' to him.

(c) This is the stage of *inspiration* or illumination. There is, as it were, a sudden flash of light, a sudden catching of one's breath. An idea has 'occurred' to him. This stage arrives unexpectedly, suddenly and is often marked by a feeling of certainty. The state of 'creative emptiness', which marked the period of incubation is suddenly filled by an answer 'as if by the grace of God'. It is therefore often accompanied by a feeling of having been passive, a mere bystander in what has occurred. Max Ernst, the painter, for instance, described this when he wrote: 'I had only to reproduce obediently what made itself visible within me.' And so logical and rational a person as the mathematician Gauss described how: 'Finally, two days ago, I succeeded, not on account of my painful efforts, but by the grace of God. Like a sudden flash of lightning the riddle happened to be solved.' And Paul Klee expressed through a most beautiful symbol this very experience of the creative process when he compared the artist to the trunk of a tree:

> From the root the sap rises up into the artist, flows through him, flows to his eyes. He is the trunk of the tree. Overwhelmed and activated by the force of the current, he conveys his vision into his work ... he does nothing other than gather and pass on what rises from the depths. He neither serves nor commands, he transmits. His position is humble. And the beauty at the crown is not his own; it has merely passed through him.

In this third phase, exuberance and ecstasy are often experienced.

(d) But the fourth stage is a sort of 'coming-down-to-earth'. It is the stage of *verification*. This is a period of critical testing, when the ideas received in the period of inspiration are tested, organised and given relevant and appropriate form and expression.

Indeed, when one examines these four stages of the creative process it becomes clear that creativity depends on a person being able both to use his ego functions and to surrender his ego functions. Inevitably ego functions must predominate in the first stage when knowledge and skill are needed and when a problem presents itself. Again, the ego functions must re-assert their predominance in the fourth stage when the gifts of 'inspiration' must be evaluated critically and work must be done with them and on them. But, during the second and the third stages the capacity to surrender ego functions and ego controls is essential. For these two stages rely on what Ehrenzweig has named 'unconscious scanning' or the 'creative suspension of frontiers'. In his *Hidden order of art* he has suggested that this process is indeed vital to all creative work. But it can only come about if a person is able to relinquish the normal compulsion to differentiate sharply and can instead allow himself to scatter his attention; and so the boundaries dissolve until everything seems 'to fuse into a single oceanic image'. Kekule, the discoverer of the benzine ring, described in an amusing manner his understanding of this necessary interaction of conscious and unconscious activity in creative work when he admonished his colleagues:

> Let us learn to dream, gentlemen—then perhaps we shall find the truth. But let us beware of publishing our dreams before they have been put to the proof by the waking understanding.

And Housman expressed the pleasure and the disappointment that he experienced in the course of the making of a poem:

> Having drunk a pint of beer—beer is a sedative to the brain and my afternoons are the least intellectual portion of my life—I would go for a walk. As I went along thinking of nothing in particular, there would flow into my mind with sudden and unaccountable emotion, sometimes a line or two of verse, sometimes a whole stanza at once, accompanied, not preceded, by a vague notion of the poem as a whole. Then there would usually be a lull and perhaps the spring would bubble up again. I say bubble up, because the source of the suggestion thus proffered to the brain was an abyss.

But then he goes on to describe an episode when the brain itself had to fill in the gaps. He sounds almost aggrieved, even if humorously so, that it had cost him some real, conscious effort:

> I happen to remember distinctly the genesis of the piece which stands last in my first volume. Two of the stanzas, I do not say which, came into my head, just as they are printed, while I was crossing the corner of Hampstead Heath between the Spaniard's Inn and the footpath to Temple Fortune. A third stanza came with a little coaxing after tea. One more was needed, but it did not come. I had to turn to and compose it myself, and that was a laborious business; I wrote it thirteen times, and it was more than twelve months before I got it right.

The preciseness with which he describes his location in space when the poem emerged from inside him is rather fascinating.

Ehrenzweig has postulated that there exist formal elements and an order that the unconscious yields spontaneously, drawing on levels that are deeper than the area which, according to psychoanalysts, originate primary process activity. Such primary processes have been thought of as producing only the raw material of man's thoughts and feelings, consisting essentially of chaotic and wild sexual and aggressive phantasies, which must then be 'tamed' by the 'secondary processes'—that is, the processes characteristic of ego-activity—before they can become either communicable or aesthetic.

As a matter of fact, Marion Milner had already forecast in 1956 that the recent researches into art and aesthetics would sooner or later call for a revision of the whole concept of the nature and function of the primary process. Such a revision is now well under way.

Ehrenzweig has, then, developed his hypothesis of a 'hidden

133

order' in the deep unconscious on the basis of considerable research. Thus, for instance, Desmond Morris's collection of ape paintings or Kellog's collection and analysis of infant scribbles, or Charles Fisher's experiments with Rubin's double profile or the musician's experience of 'horizontal' hearing, which is in fact polyphonic and occurs when attention is not focused on a single musical theme or instrument—all these and many more seem to provide evidence of an order independent of our conscious concern with differentiation and the distinction between figure and ground, inside and outside, space and time, etc.

It is this capacity to suspend ego functions and controls, to risk 'not knowing' and 'not controlling', to allow oneself, to make oneself available to possession and to the possible experience of 'sacred awe', which the poet Keats has called 'negative capability', and which he has described as the capacity to be 'in uncertainties, mysteries, doubts, without any irritable reaching after fact and reason.'

This interdependence of activity and receptivity, of control and surrender, of consciousness and unconsciousness, has been understood and conceptualised by psychoanalysts like Marion Milner and Hannah Segal when they described the creative process as: 'a genital bisexual activity, necessitating a good identification with the father who gives and the mother who receives and bears the child.'

A similar conceptualisation of the creative process also underlies Neumann's thesis that every artist is an essentially bisexual person. This has more recently been supported by MacKinnon's studies, in which she found that in a sample of architects the more creative ones scored higher on femininity than did the less successful and less creative ones.

Nor is the analogy between giving birth to a baby and creative activity the invention or discovery of modern psychologists. The poet Rilke, for instance, among many others, has talked about it in just these terms, when he described the making of a poem as: 'Like a birth which is drawn urgently out of the biological and spiritual depths of the poet'.

Schneider, in his thoughtful book *The psychoanalyst and the artist*, also emphasises the importance of the bisexual in all creative work. He there discusses the creative process as composed of what he calls a creative thrust coming from the unconscious, and creative mastery added by the ego. The psychic system that relates and so transforms these two is the pre-conscious, which, though it has no dynamic of its own, acts like the hub of a wheel. Thus the unconscious intuitive thrust combines with conscious cognitive mastery. Schneider sees this marriage of thrust and of mastery also in sexual terms and so he too emphasises the fact of heightened bisexuality in creative persons. But he thinks of the gifted person as identifying not solely with mother and father, but beyond them with the 'unseen' act, the 'unfelt' pleasure and above all with the 'inevitable result of sexual creativity', that is the child.

The importance of the theme of the child and the ease of identification with it has recently been investigated in India in relation to Indian folk painters by Renaldo Maduro. By examining 155 Hindu folk painters who had been divided into three groups by their community according to their creative qualities, he found that those in the most creative group remembered their childhood memories more clearly and more easily than did the less creative ones. In the Rorschach and in the TAT stories they used the child-image more frequently and explained that for them to create is like playing and that they feel themselves to be children. Playing implies deep absorption and is in any case highly respected in the Hindu world in which it was play, not work, that created the world during the dance of Lord Vishnu.

Maduro found that in the highly creative group were men who had

(a) a particularly rich phantasy life;
(b) could tolerate ambiguity;
(c) were capable of very complex symbolic identifications; and
(d) had more fluid and permeable outer and inner ego boundaries, with a strong ego-core, requiring less unconscious defensive manœuvres.

Their phantasies and conscious ideals involved shifting child–parent identifications, together with sexual rôle confusion and phantasies of union with the mother.

These particularly creative Hindu painters work within the symbolic images of their own culture, but they do so in unique and personalised ways. They seemed to identify both with the creator, Lord Vishvakarma, with the Divine Mother, and also with the Divine Child, Krishna. Many of them confessed that the birth and life of the divine child was one of the most important sources of their inspiration and creative work. The fact that they felt themselves to be creative artists and were accepted by their community as creative artists may further support Winnicott's contention that culture—and creativity—result from the interplay of tradition and personal originality.

Jung has often discussed the theme of the child, of the divine child—and of youth, eternal youth or the *puer aeternus*, and he has described them as archetypal because he believed them to be universally present in the human psyche. The *puer aeternus* tends to symbolise primarily beauty, strength, courage, idealism and the young hero who ventures forth in order to take on apparently impossible risks and impossible adversaries, and who despite all temptations retains intact his resoluteness and his purity. The child, on the other hand, stands for growth, development and futurity, and its presence as an inner figure means that the person has available sufficient sap and vitality for further evolution, for further creative life and even for a new beginning. Thus when these images occur they denote trust in life and in the presence of potential growing points.

Some, at least partial, identification with either of these two archetypal personages is likely to characterise a person who possesses such attributes as flexibility, playfulness, innocence, the ability to grow, to develop, to learn and who is available to experiences of wonder and awe; for such identifications help to preserve and to nurture these qualities. Madura's researches in India seem to bear this out, and they suggest that these people themselves are aware of such linkages.

In the latter part of his book, *The hidden order of art*, Ehrenzweig explored the myth of the 'dying god' also in relation to creative processes. He had been led to it by the work and the writings of Marion Milner, and in particular by studying her thoughts and experiences which she has described in *An experiment in leisure*. He came to agree with her that her images of suffering and destruction and death are indeed images and symbols of the ego's creativity, a creativity which these images both represent and also induce. He named such images 'poemagogic' and pointed out that before Marion Milner it had only been Jung who had grasped the poemagogic quality of the kind of myth and material that Frazer had collected; and he acknowledged that in developing his theory of the archetypes Jung had really pointed to those intrapsychic forces that function as guardians over certain of our creative processes, since they are truly intermediaries between the ego and the self in analogy to the 'messengers' or 'sons' or 'pieces' of God as I have argued in an earlier paper (Gordon, 1963).

Ehrenzweig's concept of the structure of the mind has curiously close affinities with those formulated in analytical psychology; thus he has postulated that there is in fact a mental level that is even below that of poemagogic imagery, a level he has described as the 'undifferentiated matrix'; here oceanic experience predominates. And he described the 'gradual descent into the oceanic depths'—essential to all creative work —at least as a possibility—as follows:

First there is the Oedipal level.

Next down is the level at which the father recedes in importance and distinctness; instead the mother acquires phallic-oral characteristics and becomes more terrifying.

Then comes the level where the mother is endowed with the full power of both parents and so threatens not just castration but death—by tearing and dismemberment.

But in the deepest level, the level of the undifferentiated matrix, the creative powers of both parents are absorbed through an identification with the divine child. To this deepest stage belong then the feelings of 'greatest stillness, austerity and serenity', which Marion Milner had experienced at the conclusion of the working through of the sado-masochistic theme of the dying god. It is from this fourth level that stem the processess of de-differentiation or unconscious scanning, and it is from this level that the 'hidden order' can emerge. But Ehrenzweig rightly insists that this fourth level cannot be genuinely attained and experienced unless and until death has been faced and the experience of dying been worked through. And he also emphasises—what has been so clear in the Indian material that Madura has collected—that in creative work the triangular Oedipal situation dissolves—at least during part of the time—so that the level of structural undifferentiation can then act as a catalyst.

Ehrenzweig makes it quite explicit that he thinks of

de-differentiation and re-differentiation as mirroring the death and the rebirth of the ego, and that this can be understood to be the result of the interaction between the basic life and the basic death instincts. He quotes in support of this hypothesis a number of writers who are clearly preoccupied with the theme of birth, death and rebirth. Otto Rank, for instance, who interpreted a vast quantity of artistic and mythological material as phantasies of undoing birth and returning to the womb, perhaps, so he thought, as an experienced image of the process of containment and expansion inherent in all creative work. Or Rilke, in his *Book of hours*, where he expresses the poet's longing for death and for creativity, which is felt as man's real motherhood. Or Robert Graves, who extracts from almost any myth the ubiquitous theme of the White Goddess, the true Muse, to whose 'killing love the poet must submit'. For in worshipping her he invites his own death in exchange for love and rebirth. Thus also, more recently, Phyllis Greenacre, who in 'The childhood of the artist' writes that 'Personally I can no more conceive of life without an intrinsic movement towards death than I can conceive of perpetual motion', and Marion Milner, who thinks of oceanic states of fusion and de-differentiation as prerequisites for successful symbol formation.

Thus through studying the process of creation and art-making Ehrenzweig has been led to postulate that:

(a) There is in the psyche an area where states of wholeness and completion predominate, both as experience and as goal.

(b) The psyche is liable to produce poemagogic images. These tend to represent the creative process and they induce the creative process.

(c) There is a death wish that seeks, through the process of de-differentiation, to re-establish experiences of fusion and wholeness.

These three processes belong to the deeply unconscious levels of the psyche. His conception of the psyche has thus remarkably close affinities with the Jungian concepts of the 'primary self', the 'archetypes' and the 'self'.

Greenacre in the above-mentioned paper, which was based on her studies of biographies, autobiographies and on her clinical experience, postulated that there might be four basic characteristics that mark, right from the beginning of life, an individual who will prove to be endowed with special creative talents. She enumerated them as follows:

1. A greater-than-average sensitivity to sensory stimulation, so that sensory experience is likely to be more extensive and also more intensive. In consequence, in the case of a gifted infant, reaction to his mother's breast may involve an intensified awareness of the breast's sensory qualities, not only its milk-giving characteristic, but also its warmth, smell, roundness of form, texture, etc. He is therefore likely to react more easily to any similar smell, touch, taste and visual sensation that happens to come his way.

2. An unusual capacity for awareness of relations between the various stimuli. Thus, the heightened sensations being accompanied by a more subtle sensibility to similarities and differences, the infant has an earlier and firmer sense of Gestalt and can therefore accept and relate more easily to substitutes of the primary objects. But having wider than average sensuous sensibility together with a greater awareness of the sensuous relationships of stimuli he may also have a greater than usual need to harmonise the world of objects with his internal objects, needs and phantasies. Thus such children often grow up into persons who can, more than the average person, see unusual relationships and combine apparently dissociated systems of experience.

Greenacre has coined the term 'collective alternates' for that 'increased range of outer objects' that can 'substitute for the warmer personal objects'. I suspect that the collective alternates are the complement to those inner, those psychic constituents, that analytical psychologists have named 'archetypes', a concept designed to account for man's capacity to experience and to relate to pre-personal and non-primary objects.

Redfearn in a paper, 'Bodily experience in psychotherapy', has described these 'pre-personal experiences' as those bodily experiences that cannot yet be referred to consistent body images with stable boundaries, for they do not yet originate from the encounter with actual external objects; rather, so he suggests, they are body experiences that tend to be projected to such boundaryless forces as wind, floods, fires, earthquakes, etc. Greenacre has explored in greater detail the sensory structure and organisation of these 'collective alternates' and she suggests that their presence can help the gifted child to reduce the traumatic effect of potentially critical situations. For instance, during the period of bowel training such a child may start earlier and with greater satisfaction to play with mud or clay as substitutes for faeces.

3. A greater-than-usual disposition to an empathy of wider range and deeper vibration. This seems to me to be indeed an important quality, for it does enrich and enliven the inner world and it encourages the empathetic animation of the inanimate world and so heightens a general responsiveness. The tendency to animate or to anthropomorphise tends in the average child to yield early to the pressures of the so-called adults in a scientific and rationalist society; but the gifted child defends himself stubbornly against such pressures and thus the objects and forms in his inner world remain fresh and alive.

4. An efficient sensorimotor equipment, which then allows him to externalise and to give tangible expression to what he experiences inside him. It is probably in just this area that education can be particularly helpful by encouraging and training the manual, motor and intellectual skills.

To summarise: the process of creation demands first and foremost that a person be available to those freely moving oscillations between control and surrender, between differentiation and de-differentiation, that is between periods of active conscious work on the one hand and periods of passive acceptance on the other. And if the creative process is to function in any of the many areas of activity—living, relating, making, discovering, inventing—then special gifts and aptitudes are almost essential assets.

In as much as the analytic process is also a creative venture, so analyst and analysand, too, are likely to experience the oscillations between activity and receptivity, and between certainty and doubt. They, too, are likely to pass through periods of 'incubation' marked by feelings of 'muddled suspense'. If they are lucky they may then be available to 'inspiration', which in that particular work-context would have to do with the discovery of some new insight or a novel experience or the emergence of a new quality in their inter-relationship.

Certainly in my work I am now quite familiar with the experience of feeling baffled, confused and unable to make sense of something, be it a dream or a particular situation that has developed in the transference–countertransference between the analysand and myself. I have learned to value these moments of bewilderment, to accept them and not battle against them, although they can, of course, be painful for both of us. But in my acceptance of this 'not-knowing', in my shedding of the mantle of omniscience and omnipotence—whether or not I verbalise this to the analysand and so make it explicit between us—I know that I may ultimately help the patient to find release from his own compulsion to cling to the known and the controllable. For my acceptance of 'not-knowing' may mediate for him the awareness that he, too, may dare to grow and to create, even though he is not in possession of perfect knowledge or perfect skill or perfect control; and so good-enoughness may come to seem good enough.

CHAPTER 2

Psychological functions in the service of the creative process

According to the *Oxford English Dictionary*, to create means to 'bring into being, to cause to exist, to form, to produce'.

Essential to this activity of making and creating is what I have called the 'urge to incarnate', or to 'make flesh'. I have already alluded to this in Part II, and to Prof. Louis Reid who, speaking in particular of the making of art, from the point of view of a philosopher of aesthetics, has also called it 'creative aesthetic embodiment'. He has in fact explored this new concept in considerable depth, and he has suggested that in such 'creative embodiment' the

> perceived sounds, shapes, rhythms, etc. are not only instrumental to the grasp of aesthetic meaning; the experience of attentive perception to them is an essential part of the apprehension of meaning. Attention to perceived forms is both instrumental and intrinsic to the understanding of aesthetic meaning. Content and medium are indivisibly and uniquely united. (Reid, p. 76)

Clearly these two concepts—'incarnation' and 'embodiment' —overlap considerably. But in the Latin form there seems to me to be implicit a greater emphasis on the element of sacrifice, and sacrifice inexorably accompanies the acceptance of the limits and limitations that impose themselves when the abstract or the ideal is given form, that is body.

The urge to 'embody' or to 'incarnate' rests on the fact that we sensate and we dream, and we always live at the same time in a world of objects and in a world of meanings. Thus, inevitably, we carry inside us the desire to bring these two worlds together. And while, on the one hand, we always search for more and more adequate forms through which to express the ever-changing world of our sensuous experiences, we also

Psychological functions in the service of the creative process

strive always to imbue with meaning and significance the sensuous forms that we encounter. Thus man has always been driven to attempt to clothe his internal images in forms existing outside him; and this in order (a) to relate as much as possibe of what goes on inside him to the outer world; (b) to conserve in some tangible form for himself, in the future, his present experiences; and (c) to communicate and even to commune with others, so as to achieve moments when he can shed awareness of his separateness and share with others some significant and possibly ineffable experience.

While the giving of form to an inner experience is joyous and fulfilling, yet it also carries with it disappointment and sadness, for the work can hardly ever match the excitement of the moment of inspiration or the pleasurable absorption during the process of making. As James Hillman has put it:

> We experience our relation to the opus as both fulfilment and suffering; fulfilment because through the opus the creative is contained and realised [and hence, I would add, in a form in which it can be shared and communicated], suffering because the limitation of each opus, each field, tragically limits the creative possibility to the confines of actual realisation ... From the beginning the opus determines my relation to it. It presents me with my sacrifice and constellates the creative suffering from the beginning. (Hillman: *Art International*, XIII, 7, 1969, p. 27)

Marion Milner expressed in relevant body language this same dilemma when she wrote in *On not being able to paint* that inevitably the infant experiences a disappointing discrepancy between the excitement of the process of defecation and its produce, the faeces.

The tragedy inherent in incarnation has only rarely been expressed in any post-mediaeval paintings of the nativity, as has recently been pointed out—both verbally and in an actual painting—by an American artist, Brenda Bettinson. And yet the uniqueness of the story of Christ lies in its very emphasis that the Spirit, the Word, had become flesh and was thus subject to pain and suffering and death; and that therefore his birth is the occasion not only for rejoicing but also for mourning.

The seriousness and the commitment with which artists, and even creative scientists, speak about their work suggests to me that man's creative activity has much in common with religious and mystical experience. One of the essential features that characterise both mystics and creative persons is the passionate need to find meaning, not just facts. This seems to evolve from man's desire to find some order and unity behind the discontinuities of the world of objects and stimuli, to discover some sort of significance in order to make sense of the immediacy and above all of the transitoriness, of actual experience. But artists and mystics share a greater than average capacity to experience wonder and awe. Their availability to these experiences implies that they have sacrificed enough of their need for personal omnipotence, and hence they can risk the awareness that there might indeed exist something mysterious and unknowable—whether this be located inside them or outside them—which eludes control and manipulation. Einstein has expressed with great beauty and lucidity just this particular feeling:

> The most beautiful emotion we can experience is the mystical. It is the sower of all true art and science. To know that what is impenetrable to us really exists, manifesting itself with the highest wisdom and most radiant beauty which our dull faculties can comprehend only in their most primitive forms–this knowledge, this feeling is at the centre of true religiousness and art.

There are also undeniably qualities that differentiate the mystic from the creative artist or scientist. For instance, the mystic's primary concern is to achieve the experience of fusion and union with 'the All', 'the Absolute', 'the Godhead'; in other words he strives and he longs for what Freud had called the 'oceanic experience'. With him passivity preponderates and he tends to shun matter, sensation, the sensuous, that is, *form*. In this he is most essentially different from the creative person. And the artist is in fact most precariously poised between the need for fusion on the one hand and the excitement and the pain of separateness and differentiation on the other. Harold Rugg, for instance, when speaking of Blake as the forerunner of Coleridge, Whitman and Bergson, describes how these men followed the intuitive path in their acts of partial withdrawal from the physical world, but then, instead of continuing that path to the point of final union with the Absolute, they undertook to 'endure the ordeal of return'. Thus they strove to bring together the sensory with the intuitive and the temporal with the eternal.

This 'ordeal of return' was expressed clearly and dramatically in the dream of the young and gifted artist whom I have already described in Part I, Chapter 1. For when he told me of the last part of his dream, in which he saw his art school, the patient broke down and wept bitterly—which expressed a mixture of sadness at losing heaven and joy at finding his art school.

Another artist, a successful painter and engraver, who had for many years been interested in Indian philosophy and meditation, dreamed the following dream:

> I am going to see a wise Indian, a sort of guru. I want to bring him a present. I have a lump of some brown, semi-soft stuff in my hand, but then I think it is not the appropriate sort of thing to give him. So I leave it behind . . . It is rather like a lump of shit.

After cogitating about it for some time, she suddenly remarked, 'Perhaps it is even more like a lump of clay or Plasticine.' Thus she too battled with the conflict whether to enter into the experience of the void, the formless or whether to return to her craft, her concern with matter.

It is in his will-to-form, in the valuing of his senses and in his fascination with the sensuous world around him, that the creative person differs so essentially from the mystic. Far from trying to sacrifice body to spirit, the artist or the scientist tries to relate them to one another and to discover in what way they might be inter-related. In consequence, the perceptual and the psychological processes, through which he is related to the world of matter, are of particular importance to him.

Perception, however, is not itself just a passive receptor mechanism and the visual apparatus does not function like a camera or the auditory apparatus like a tape-recorder. Instead, as Arnheim has expressed it,

> . . . far from being merely passive registrations, perceptions are creative acts of grasping structure even beyond the mere grouping and selecting of parts . . . Perceiving is abstracting in that it represents individual cases through configurations of general categories.

The study of the perceptual processes has therefore shown the mind's tendency to make figures and shapes, to gloss over apparently irrelevant gaps and to produce the best possible interpretation of any given sensory data. We can therefore never see the world just as it is; rather, the way we see the world is determined by a combination of its actual qualities plus the information, expectation and needs of the percipient.

Clearly imagery is one of the most important influences that affect the organising principle of perception. I have defined an 'image' as:

> The perception of sensory data like forms, colours, sounds, smells, movements, objects, etc. in the absence of an actual external stimulus that could have caused such perception. This does not mean that such external stimuli have never been present in the past, nor that an image is independent of such past experience. But it does mean that at the time when the image occurs no such stimulus is present. (Gordon: 'A very private world')

Imagery seems to be a universal phenomenon in man—and possibly also in animals, as the work of the ethologists suggests. Certainly in the case of man imagery enables him to classify, to abstract, and to relate his present perceptions to past experience. Through imagery man is helped to bear present frustrations for the sake of some future satisfaction.

But a great many variables characterise imagery; this differentiates one person's image-world from that of another. Yet because images are all-pervasive in the psyche of man, because they enfold him like a mantle, they often elude introspection and make awareness of their very presence difficult. Furthermore, unlike thoughts that can find expression in words, images cannot be validated, for there is no way in which they can be communicated directly. Language and discursive thought are unequal to such a task.

Through art forms man can, however, to some extent at least, break the seal that locks him into his inner world. For art is the language that least distorts his image world and is, as nearly as his skill will allow, analogous to it. The privacy of the image world on the one hand, together with man's need to communicate and to validate this inner world, is probably one of the most powerful incentives that drives man to make art.

Image and imagination are two terms that are often used interchangeably, in popular language. That is a pity; for though they have clearly an etymological link, yet they refer to different psychological processes. An image is a representation of a sensuous and individual experience. It is the raw material of 'imagination'. In imagination images have been assembled together, they have been dramatised, they have been 'produced' so that they tell a story which has not only cognitive content but above all emotional urgency and meaning. In other words the image in relation to imagination is like a still picture in relation to a moving film. Imagination in the absence of images is impossible; and equally creation without imagination is unthinkable.

Of course one of the most essential functions in the creative process is symbolisation, which I have discussed in some detail in Part II. While I was writing this part of the book I came across a Zen saying that seems to sum up what I try to convey when I talk about symbolising:

> Before one practises Zen, mountains are mountains and trees are trees; that is to say, there is only the reality of the reality of the relative world. But after one has practised Zen for some time mountains are no longer mountains and trees are no longer trees; one has seen the absolute underlying unity of all things. But at the completion of one's practice of Zen, mountains are again mountains and trees trees.

Creative work in the arts in particular depends on the capacity to live—almost simultaneously—in two or even more realities, the internal and the external, the personal and the collective, the conscious and the unconscious; and it is in the creative arts that experience at the symbolic and experience at the pre-symbolic level may in fact coincide. I have already pointed this out when I suggested that an artist may at times, during the creative work, function in terms of symbolic equation, that is he may then cease to operate in terms of the 'as if' attitude; though in order to complete the work he will have to return to an acknowledgment of existence of both outer as well as inner reality. Such awareness tends to be communicated through certain ritualised artistic conventions. Thus the frame around the picture proclaims that the reality inside the picture is different and separate from the reality of the wall on which it is displayed. Equally the convention of the stage which, as it were, 'frames' a play announces that what occurs 'there' is 'true' in a different sense from that of everyday life. For the essence of what is inside the frame or on the stage is really what Winnicott has termed 'the illusion',

> ... that which is allowed to the infant, and which in adult life is inherent in art and religion, and yet becomes the hallmark of madness when an adult puts too powerful a claim on the credulity of others, forcing them to acknowledge a sharing of illusion that is not their own. We can share a respect of illusory experience, and if we wish we may collect together and form a group on the basis of the similarity of our illusory experiences. This is a natural root of grouping among human beings. (Winnicott, 1971)

The madman, we may then say, is he who fails to experience and to recognise the complexity of the different 'realities', and so, in a way, he loses them all. The artist on the other hand exposes himself to the experience of the dynamic tension of the different realities; this can be exhausting, even if exciting. Consequently in both personal and cultural history there is always a constant shifting of the balance, now towards outer reality and the reassurance of the existence of the past, of the collective and of tradition—this can degenerate to formalism or even mannerism; now towards the inner world and the potential fascination with the purely private and thence the abstruse, perhaps even the absurd and grotesque. Should outer reality be experienced as too unsatisfactory or as a threat to personal identity, imagination may be used as a refuge and as a substitute for reality rather than as a means of enlivening it. And so the frame may be discarded and the stage may be broken up; and what might have been symbolic enrichment will develop into concretisation and fetishism. Instead of a creative artist we shall find a Walter Mitty; and there will be a clamorous demand that God be tangible, or else an equally clamorous assertion that He is.

In other words unless a person can be in touch with the outer world, the inner world and the area of experience—even if not always simultaneously—he will be crippled in his capacity to create or even to play. For play, as I have argued in Part II, is now seen as firmly based on the evolution of the process of symbolisation, and, as Winnicott has pointed out, directly continuous with cultural experience and hence also with creativity.

I have for some time puzzled about what might be the intrinsic characteristic of play, and what difference there might be between play and creation, if any. I have come to think that what distinguishes play from other activities is its function in terms of personality and growth. This is not to say that other activities do not also contribute to personal growth, but in their case personal growth is secondary to the actual purpose of the activity. For many activities may in themselves be the same whether they are work or play. But when they are work, their own purpose is primary, while in the case of play personal growth is the primary goal. One has only to think of those various play and leisure activities—be it children or adults who are involved—where there is really quite a lot of pain, hardship anguish and even terror. Sailing 'for fun' on storm-tossed seas, sitting for hours fishing, listening to ghost stories in the dark, playing 'cops and robbers' and even 'peekaboo'. Essential to all these seems to be the attempt to increase experience—of the inanimate world, of the animate world, of the world of one's fellow humans or of one's own private world.

Play then, I believe, is above all in the service of the process of individuation, in the sense in which Jung has used this term. As I understand it, especially as it has been developed and elaborated by Michael Fordham, individuation comprises readiness for ever greater awareness of one's own nature, with its positive and negative sides, and an ever sharper definition of who and what one is; this is then reflected in the clarity and in the appropriateness of one's self-image, a recognition of one's separateness and personal responsibility, together with, and in the context of, an acceptance of the existence of patterns and processes that exist beyond our control and comprehension. In other words, for me at least, individuation encompasses 'individualisation', but it moves a person beyond this essentially ego-building process towards the search for values and meaning and self-transcendence.

When play evolves into an act of creation, then, I would postulate, though very tentatively, a person has reached the point where he tries to transcend even his urge for ego-growth and individualisation in order to put himself also at the service of such self-transcending values as truth, beauty, spirit and the search for meaning. Thus, through creativity a person searches out the experience of communication and of communion, and he strives to forge links inside himself between the ego and the self, the personal and the collective, the here-and-now and the transcendent.

If I were to end this chapter here I might be accused of idealising the creative process and of being rather starry-eyed about it. I have, however, emphasised throughout, particularly when I discussed the stages of the creative process, that creation is 'work' and entails also the down-to-earth activities of perception, attention, skill and critical judgment that characterise stages 1 and 4; without them creativity would remain unembodied. Perhaps my point of view has been expressed most aptly and most poetically by W. H. Auden, when, basing himself on Coleridge, he elaborated the idea of the primary and the secondary imagination:

> The concern of the Primary Imagination, its only concern, is with sacred beings and sacred events ... A sacred being cannot be anticipated, it must be encountered ... The impression made by a sacred event is of an overwhelming but undefinable significance. The Secondary Imagination is of another character and at another mental level. It is active, not passive ... Secondary Imagination is social and craves agreement with other minds ... Both kinds of imagination are essential to the life and health of the mind. Without the inspiration of sacred awe, its beautiful forms would soon become banal, its rhythms mechanical; without the activity of the Secondary Imagination the passivity of the Primary would be the mind's undoing; sooner or later its sacred beings would possess it, it would come to think of itself as sacred, exclude the outer world as profane and so go mad ... The value of a profane thing lies in what it usefully does, the value of a sacred thing lies in what it *is*.

So wrote Auden in 1956 in his paper 'Making, knowing and judging', and I am grateful to Masud Khan for having brought this valuable paper to my attention.

To summarise: the qualities that the creative person needs to possess—be he artist, scientist, mystic, or someone whose creativity is expressed in the way he lives his life and relates to others—is bound up with the deep-seated need to find meaning, not just facts. It is also inseparable from the willingness to make himself available to experiences of surprise, of awe, of wonder. For only the person who can tolerate the awareness that there exists both inside him and outside him something mysterious that transcends his capacity to control and to manipulate, only he dare expose himself to these feelings.

Furthermore, the creative person, perhaps more than anybody else, is exposed to the temptation either to remain quite passive, waiting dreamily for 'inspiration' to transpierce him, or else to insist on solving the creative task entirely through his own conscious and controllable functions and skills. Alternatively he may demote art into a sort of handmaiden to his personal quirks, using it to express himself, that is his little personal self, the ego, and so that it performs the function of a therapy.

In other words, in order to create, a person needs to be aware of and to affirm his personal characteristics, history and idiosyncrasies and yet hold himself available to experience sudden moments of inspiration, illumination, possession, vision.

CHAPTER 3

Hindrances to the creative process

If we accept Jung's hypothesis that in man the drive to create is in fact instinctive—that is innate—then we must postulate that like all other instincts the creative instinct also is subject to vicissitudes, distortions and obstructions as a result of one or other psychological conflict.

And if it is true that in the creative process the forces of life and death are interacting particularly closely, then it cannot be surprising that the conflicts evoked during creative work might be particularly sharp and daunting. After all, to discover and to make something new demands courage and the ability to bear doubt and pain and all the anxieties that are provoked when one jettisons what is old and familiar and risks innovation—that is, the forming of something new, something as yet unknown. Prometheus incurred the wrath of Zeus for just that, and in consequence suffered the agony the God saw fit to impose—the daily devouring of his liver—that organ generally associated with fortitude and bravery.

What personality characteristics or psychological conflicts might prove to be particularly unfavourable to the functioning of the creative process? The following come to mind because I have encountered them personally both inside and outside the consulting room:

Excessive narcissism, for instance, can seriously interfere with the creative process; for narcissism—or what is even worse, delusions of omnipotence and omniscience—can seriously cripple the capacity to test and to evaluate one's work and one's inspiration. They also discourage recognition of one's dependence on the knowledge and information gained and made available by other people, by other epochs, and by other cultures. Instead we tend in these cases to encounter haste, impatience and a general lack of persistence, commitment

151

or devotion, in other words all qualities that mark the 'butter-fly mind' of the dilettante. Such qualities tend to interfere with the work to be done in stages 1 and 4 of the creative process.

Other characteristics can make stages 2 and 3 difficult to attain or to use. Thus the need to be always in control and carefully aware of all that goes on is likely to abort any creative work, much like the impatient cook who cannot let the cake rise peacefully inside the oven but needs to peep at it and so make it collapse. Of course such a need may repose on any number of unconscious fears and phantasies. There may, for instance, be a general fear of undifferentiation and terror of the unknown due, as Anna Freud has suggested, to disbelief that the psyche contains spontaneous ordering forces and that they are truly intrinsic to it. Or there may be a dread of the possible disappointment that the object created may turn out not to be as good or as fabulous as the excitement experienced at the moment of inspiration. Again there may be distrust in the 'good-enoughness' of one's own inner world and the suspicion that it contains forces so dangerous and so destructive that, if externalised, they would wreak disaster or provoke revenge. Or the obstacle may present itself in an exaggerated depend-ence on other people's judgment, which brings in its wake great apprehension lest the work that one has drawn out of the very depth of one's self might in fact evoke ridicule and dis-missal rather than admiration and praise.

Again, excessive narcissism and delusions of omnipotence and omniscience may prevent a person from ever attempting to incarnate his visions. For the fear that the work achieved may not be as dazzling and as sublime as one hopes and dreams may tempt him—or her—to take refuge in the elaboration of pro-jects and plans and preparations. These are, however, never taken 'to term' and given birth. In many cases the creative forces turn against their owner and, instead of work, they un-leash illness, often in the form of inventive and bizarre symp-toms. Thus the marriage of the creative forces with omni-potence and omniscience may find no better satisfaction than triumph over the puzzlement and confusion, the errors and dis-appointments of many different specialists in the medical profession.

Basic and underlying the various potential hindrances to the creative process is the capacity to trust. It is a quality that Plaut has described as essential to all play and imagination; and Winnicott in his 'Location of cultural experience' has confirmed Plaut's thesis and underpinned it in terms of his theory that the roots of art, religion and culture lie in the transitional object and in the establishment of the third area in the mind.

This capacity to trust must of course be available in more than one direction. Thus there must be some trust that there is an inner world and that this world is neither empty nor sterile. Then there must be trust that the source of creation will continue to flow and that the mind and its workings, unlike a bank account that is exhausted if one uses the assets, are more like a spring: that it will go on flowing and perhaps flow the better the more one draws on it. Again there must be enough trust so that the constructive, the synthesising, the loving forces are sufficiently strong to contain and to balance the destructive and hating forces inside one. And there must be enough trust so that omnipotence and the will for mana and magic have been sufficiently curbed so that the limitations of being only (not more than) human have come to be accepted and even valued.

Then there must be enough trust that the world and the people inside it exist, are relatively reliable and benevolent and relatively free from excessive envy—thus leading one to expect minimal persecution, thieving or destructive criticism. But the world and its people must also be felt as sufficiently solid and sufficiently able to resist one's own lurking destructiveness or wish for domination.

And finally there must be enough trust that the third area —that is, the area of experience and of illusion—has been sufficiently differentiated and established, so that there is little danger that the illusions might over-run and drive out awareness of either the external or the internal realities; little danger, in other words, that the achievement of symbolisation with its 'as if' attitude might be permanently and completely lost. For then the visitations of the unconscious phantasies would indeed turn into unwelcome guests, squatters, that is obsessions that could turn the would-be creator into the madman.

Thus an analysis of the sort of trusting essential to the creative process shows it to be required in three basic ways: (a) trust in the good-enoughness and receptivity of the outer world; (b) trust in the existence and good-enoughness of the inner world; and (c) trust in the sufficiently reliable differentiation of the mind into the three areas of awareness.

This same sort of trust is also a prerequisite between analyst and analysand for it affects and determines in great measure the nature and the characteristics of the analytic work. Thus a patient, for instance, needs to develop enough trust that the analyst will not abandon him, rob him, destroy him, impinge on him or leave him excessively vulnerable. From his side the analyst needs to be able to trust the patient—trust that there is in him sufficient capacity for healing; trust him to use interpretations as best he can, being neither so excessively cowardly and intolerant of pain that he vomits them out irresponsibly, nor so diffident and overawed that he swallows them whole and uncritically. Rather is the analyst helped if he can trust that the patient's mental 'digestive system' functions sufficiently well so that it will in fact increase in efficiency and that in the meantime he can trust the patient to do the analytic work in his *own* time and as best he can. Such trust will guard the analyst from delusions of omnipotence or omniscience even at times when the patient may or may need to project these on to his analyst, which could provoke a *folie à deux*. Furthermore, it will prevent the analyst from regarding the patient as a walking assemblage of psychological 'mechanisms', which he can manipulate, control, engineer and predict with absolute accuracy.

Like all creative work, analysis also can be viewed as an analogue of sexual activity. The analyst giving his interpretations may, at that moment, assume the rôle of the male partner who entrusts his sperm—the interpretation—to his female partner—the patient. Neither of them can know immediately what has happened to the sperm, whether fertilisation has taken place or not. And so both must be able to wait and to trust one another, and also trust that if a new creation has been set afoot it will be good enough. At other times, in fact at most other times, the rôles are reversed; and it is the patient who gives and the analyst who receives and if possible 'takes to term' the reflections, feelings and confidences entrusted to him.

A brief description of two of my patients, each in a different sort of danger in relation to the creative process, may clarify some of the points I have tried to make and, as it were, put flesh and blood around the bones of theory.

The first is a young Scotsman, of working-class origin, whose parents had tried to 'better' themselves. He was a gifted artist who managed to function as a freelance designer. Sandy belonged—at least peripherally—to the young, *avant-garde* hippie group. His hair was long—to hide his big ears, he told me. He was slightly built; his face was gentle, almost feminine. He was not a homosexual, but was often teased as if he were one —by his enemies, by what used then to be called the 'skinheads'. In fact, a few weeks before he started analysis he was beaten up by such a gang.

Sandy had been on a few LSD trips. But from there he moved on to an interest in Zen and in the I Ching. He then began to study Jung and also joined a meditation centre. One of his uncles was a schizophrenic.

When he first came to me he was hallucinated, but had some insight into it. The voices he heard were those of his parents and near family members, and they tended to express markedly sadistic feelings and intentions towards him.

He dreamed a great deal. Most of the dreams were very detailed and they were often filled with violence and torture, and with themes of dismemberment; in some of these dreams the head is torn off the body. The violence in his dreams was sometimes perpetrated against him; at other times it was perpetrated by him; often it was just observed by the dream ego. The scene of very many of his dreams was his own home town; and although the characters in his dreams were often mythological characters—Dracula, spirits, goddesses, etc.—his parents, his sister and his grandparents also figured largely, as indeed did his childhood life, as well as the more archetypal phantasies.

In the first important dream he brought to analysis Sandy is, together with another man, a warder in a Gothic-type dungeon. They take a prisoner down into it. This is, he says, the worst dungeon they have and nobody can emerge from it. It is wet and cold and dark and large. He feels no personal animosity to the prisoner, he is just doing his duty. They chain the prisoner on to a high ledge, just next to a trickle of water from a pipe. The torture consists in the fact that the water is slowly rising; after a few days it will drown the prisoner. The prisoner re-affirms that he will not reveal his secrets; but he asks them to stay near by, just in case he changes his mind.

In the next part of the dream Sandy sees himself walk across a 'green' with his 'wife' (he was in fact not married). Suddenly they both remember the prisoner, and so they run back.

But the prison is now a library, which specialises in psychology and magic. It is also the headquarters of a spy ring. The spies are there and they try to stop him coming in. But Sandy holds them at bay with a toy gun.

Then he sees a platform and on it sit several spirits—they are like round, gleaming objects. Sandy jumps on to this platform and manages to disconnect the mechanism that makes the water drip into the dungeon. And so he saves the prisoner.

This dream seemed to characterise Sandy's wish to spy on and to extort the secrets from his unconscious—the prisoner. But he was also tempted to turn his back on his unconscious and so to forget it altogether. The final part of his dream held out the hope that he might in fact develop a respect for it and a working relationship with it.

The turning point in Sandy's analysis came when he produced the 'gates of heaven' dream, which I have recounted earlier—the dream in which he and his mother/analyst get to the threshold of heaven but, complying with the prohibition, they do not enter it. Instead, they turn back and on their homeward journey they see Sandy's art school. Thus in that dream Sandy showed a capacity to remain aware of both the temporal and the eternal, the personal and the absolute, and he seemed now willing to 'endure the ordeal of return'.

Sandy was able to terminate treatment a few months after that dream. He had become able to continue his work as an artist without feeling that he was on the threshold of madness. The hallucinations had stopped long ago and the flood of dreams had slowed down. His face assumed a firmer and more masculine quality, his general bearing was more self assured; he no longer needed to hide his 'big ears'. And his relationships both with seniors—teachers and potential employers—as well as with his contemporaries had become easier and more trusting.

In my own mind I have often compared and contrasted him with another patient, Bob who brought as his first dream the following:

> Our cat is all of a sudden going to have her kittens. I pat her back and she stands over a sort of big plate. While she stands there she starts shitting. It is in big fairly solid lumps. In the lumps I see what look like two or

three Viennese sausages and other messy bits of undigested food. Then, following directly on the lumps of shit, kittens come out, perhaps three or four of them. After the first one comes out, it drops down into the plate; but the cat does not even lick it, or give it milk. I wonder whether it will die, since it has not been licked, but it does not. All the kittens survive, but they have nothing to eat but the liquid which is in the plate, the bitter liquid that may have separated out of the shit. The kittens lick it up; they are still covered over with the sort of tissue in which they came out. In the meantime, one kitten has gone off by itself, over to the other side of the room.

Bob was an active homosexual, who looked very much younger than his years. One of his reasons for coming into analysis was that he desperately wanted to reach his own creative centre. But he was given to much ruminating and also found it difficult to commit himself to anything—be it in action, in feeling or in aesthetic judgment. He knew that he was hypercritical both of himself and of other people, but was for a long time unable to moderate it.

The triumphant manner in which he used at times to tell me of his hurts and his failures seemed an expression of his masochistic self-attack and conveyed his conviction that really he was but a piece of shit.

In fact when he first started analysis he was unable to urinate in the presence of any other person. While at school he had been terrified of the school lavatory—it seems indeed to have been a very primitive affair. His terror of this place made him have several shaming accidents at school, but it also caused him to have a recurrent dream in which each child had its own individual and enclosed W.C. cubicle instead of a desk.

There was a recurrent dream in which he is to undergo an operation in order that some nasty, dirty, smelly and poisonous stuff can be drained out of his body. There had also been a dream of babies blocking up a sewer, of self-castration because he could not, like his 'dream friend', 'ejaculate into his penis', and in one dream he felt himself to be pregnant; this last dream ended with his finding himself alone and banished to a cold and isolated cottage.

He suffered from a great deal of inertia, and could rarely complete a task because he always tended to be side-tracked by attention to details.

For a long time his analysis seemed to be stuck. Obsessional rumination continued and he got deeply involved in a relationship in which his partner—apparently through a process of projective identification—had come to collude with his own inner saboteur; for, like his own saboteur, the partner also ridiculed him, denigrated all his efforts and achievement and so confirmed his conviction that he was clueless, inefficient, indecisive, uncreative and unsociable. Both of us began to despair.

We decided to complement analysis with art therapy. The result was surprising: his paintings were quite unexpectedly free, colourful and very lively, at times humorous, at times full of terror and at times full of fun and excitement. But for several months Bob brought me his enchanting works without having any apparent emotional *rapport* with them. He could not feel the feelings they expressed, he could not 'own' them and he seemed quite cut off from the parts inside himself that had created them. But at least I had now a token of their existence. I was once more ready to persevere. Slowly the ice began to melt; slowly the barriers broke; slowly his body, his face, his voice became more animated. He could no longer remain in his limbo, he could no longer remain safely cut off from the sources of life and feeling by censorious controls and ego-defences.

The two cases I have described very briefly may help, I hope, to illustrate my thesis. For in the case of Sandy the power and seductiveness of the unconscious phantasies led to a real danger that the ego might disintegrate and that re-differentiation and the re-making of the third area, the area of the 'as if' of the symbolic process, might prove impossible.

But in the case of Bob the difficulty of surrendering ego controls and allowing a certain amount of de-differentiation obstructed his access to the creative area inside him. And so he remained for a long time like a beggar, like an impotent supplicant at the door of his own inner world, unable to get inside and unable to relinquish this quest and go elsewhere.

In other words, the hindrances to creative work and to creative living may stem either from the temptation to be caught up in non-ego processes—that is, in the forces and phantasies that stem from the self—which may then be idealised, or else the hindrance may come from an excessive distrust of the non-ego forces. Thus creativity does indeed seem to depend on the capacity to have and to tolerate the ebb and flow, the rhythm and the oscillations between conscious and unconscious, between control and surrender, between ego and non-ego.

CHAPTER 4

Death, creation and transformation: their intra-psychic interdependence

Inevitably I am now led to ask the question: can a person create—be he artist, scientist, analysand or analyst—if he represses awareness of death and if he fails to grapple with the making of some sort of conscious attitude towards it?

The intimate link between the death experience on the one hand and creativity on the other has often been discussed by Jung in terms of the psychological experience of transformation. Its expression in the social, cultural and religious fields has been much studied by anthropologists and historians of religion. Mysterious initiation rites seem to exist everywhere, and they almost always enact the symbolism of a death and a new birth. This is often ritualised in an almost literal and concretistic way. For example, among certain peoples in Melanesia and Polynesia the candidate for initiation is buried or laid in a freshly dug grave, or kept in a dark hut outside the village. His rebirth is then enacted, and frequently the neophyte must kneel between the mother's legs or appear as if spewed from the mouth of a monster. As Mircea Eliade has said: 'The scenario for initiates—whether they be candidates for a new age group, for a cult or for shamanship—is always the same: it is suffering, torture, death—and resurrection'.

Since death is one link in the chain of transformation, it tends to be experienced as a paradox, for every change or transformation involves both birth and death. Thus the death of one cell is the birth of two new cells. Indeed in the case of the unicellular organism, Eros and Thanatos function at the same moment; whichever of these changes one selects as primary will depend on where one's concern lies: with the death of the single cell or with the birth of the new cells.

It is perhaps no accident that those analysts who have been most interested in art and play and creativity have also been those who have been most ready to accept the existence of Thanatos, that is an inherent concern with and readiness for death. I am here thinking not only of the pioneers like Freud and Jung who perceived this problem many decades before others were ready to even concede that there was a problem to perceive, but I am also thinking of recent analysts like Marion Milner, Donald Winnicott and Phyllis Greenacre among several others. Greenacre, for instance, who has been quite particularly concerned with the study of the gifted child and the potential artist, has also declared quite boldly and explicitly that she can no more conceive of life without an intrinsic movement towards death than she can conceive of perpetual motion.

I believe that there has been in recent years an interaction and a reciprocity between the studies of creativity and art on the one hand and the theoretical and clinical developments in the field of analysis and psychotherapy on the other.

Both Freud and Jung had shown their interest in art, for both had drawn attention to the unconscious roots of art and they had helped to decipher some of the symbolic codes embedded there.

Jung had actually put forward a theory of art. He postulated that a work of art may be either in the 'psychological' or in the 'visionary' mode. Art in the 'psychological' mode, he suggested, was any work that stemmed predominantly from the artist's need to express and to resolve some obsessive personal conflict; consequently it did not transcend the bounds of psychological intelligibility. But art in the 'visionary' mode he claimed, was 'in-formed' by contents from the 'hinterland' of man's mind, was therefore 'sublime, pregnant with meaning, yet chilling the blood with its strangeness'. It had therefore escaped from the limitations of the personal. Instead it had 'soared beyond the personal concerns of its creator'.

In the light of more recent thinking Jung's two categories need to be re-assessed and refined, because our understanding of the interaction and interdependence of the collective and the personal unconscious has become more discriminating. In particular, Mary Williams has advanced our understanding about their interaction in her article, 'The indivisibility of the personal and the collective unconscious' in which she advanced the following two hypotheses:

First: nothing in the personal experience needs to be repressed unless the ego feels threatened by its archetypal power; and second: The archetypal activity which forms the individual's myth is dependent on material supplied by the personal unconscious. (*J. analyt. Psychol.*, **8,** 1)

In more recent years Renaldo Maduro, an analytical psychologist coming from the discipline of anthropology, has reinforced this point when he writes that:

It is necessary to point out once more that archetypes are not determined as regards their content, but only as regards their form and then only to a very limited degree. A primordial image is determined as to its content only when it has become conscious and is therefore filled out with the material of conscious experience. Its form, however, might perhaps be compared to the axial system of a crystal which, as it were, preforms the crystalline structure in the mother liquid, although it has no material existence of its own.

Until recently, however, analysts have on the whole contributed more to our understanding of art in terms of its contents rather than in terms of its formal qualities.

Students of the creative process from their side seem to have affected analytic thought and ethos. Some analysts, for instance, have come to value anew their patient's experience of silence and of aloneness (not to be confused with loneliness) and they have turned away from 'adjustment' as the goal of analytic practice and therapy. Instead they have developed a new respect for *The privacy of the self*—the title of Masud Khan's collected works. In consequence they have started to re-explore the effectiveness, during certain stages of the analysis, of such procedures as non-intervention and 'un-interpreting'. In this context I am thinking once more of analysts like Milner, Winnicott, Khan and also Balint and Little, all analysts who have shown particularly great interest in creativity. It may be that their interest, understanding and study of creativity has led them to recognise the value of the less active, less conscious and less controlling phases of that process and that this has had a feed-back effect upon their ideas about technique in analysis. Of course Freud himself was already intuitively aware of it when he recommended the adoption of an 'evenly-hovering attention' in which 'all conscious exertion' is withheld from the capacity for attention. Certainly in my own case I know and recognise how much my analytic work and my thoughts about analytic technique owe to and have been influenced by the introspections of artists and the researches of students of the creative process.

In recent decades there has unfortunately developed a tendency to think of creativity as indistinguishable from morbidity. In consequence creative people have sometimes come to think of themselves as suffering from some kind of illness.

It is, of course, true that people in the throes of a creative work often suffer from moods of irritability, depression, sadness, despair, and sometimes they seem to live out the actual themes of death, dying and torture. Such moods are often characteristic of the 'incubation' period and can be evidence that the person experiences that 'creative suspension of frontiers', that process of 'unconscious scanning', which is probably the most difficult stage in the creative process. Anybody who has experienced them or, what is almost worse, who has lived beside someone who happens to be going through such a phase, will know how painful, uncomfortable, frustrating and irritating such a period can be. What makes it worse, of course, is that one can never, while one is in the middle of it, know whether this is really the announcement of a period of creative activity, or whether it is merely a gratuitous, and less beneficent, if not actually malignant, regression. For, just as one cannot cheat death by clinging with delusionary certainty to the idea of rebirth, so one cannot cheat in the creative process by accepting disorientation as the inevitable forerunner of an inspiration.

The linkage of creativity with morbidity has also tempted some neurotics to idealise their neurosis and to believe that their neurosis is in fact art or at least the source of art. As early as 1924 Jung had drawn attention to this confusion. It is, I suppose, a hang-over of the Romantic Movement, which became dominant and influential at the beginning of the Industrial Revolution and which idealised emotionalism and personal isolation. Perhaps it was a natural compensation— perhaps a prophetic reaction—to the rationalism, the technicalisation and the collectivisation that, inevitably, followed in the wake of the Industrial Revolution.

Nevertheless we must remain aware that the depths from which he draws his inspiration, and the need to set aside ego controls, at least temporarily, in the course of the creative process, can expose a person to real risks to his psychological balance. This is particularly so in an age where ritual and religious beliefs have lost their power over men, where social institutions are breaking apart—thus depriving individuals of their known social rôles—and where the rapid developments in technology render skills obsolete within a short space of time. The individual therefore often finds himself isolated and alone in the presence of forces emerging from that archetypal—or poemagogic—level of the psyche that provides such powerful material for the imagination. To be in their grip can indeed be an ecstatic as well as a horrific and terrifying experience, precisely because the archetypal images or themes are 'deintegrates' out of the undifferentiated matrix of the self; usually they have not yet become re-integrated into the ego structure, with its emphasis on reality testing and as its principal function the perception and organisation of responses relevant to both external and internal stimuli. Because they are still imbued with an aura of 'otherness' of 'not-I', they tend to be experienced as super-personal, as overwhelming, and so they can indeed create states of crisis and of ego disintegration.

The value of creativity and the value of death for the survival and the evolution of the species, as well as for the growth and continuing development of the individual, should be obvious by now. There is a simple but telling tale in the storehouse of Chinese folklore:

A young emperor was wandering around his gardens accompanied by several members of his retinue. He delighted in all the beauty that met his eye: the trees, the shrubs, the flowers, the buds, the birds, the timid deer, the colourful fishes in his ponds. But suddenly a shadow of sadness passed over his face; gladness left him; he sighed. 'To think that one day I will die and then I will lose all this', he murmured. One of his courtiers overheard this; he approached the emperor gently and whispered, 'Sire, if there were no death, this palace and these gardens would not be yours. Your ancestor would still be here.'

Some of the African stories of the origin of death betray a similar understanding.

Creativity is also essential, particularly in the case of the more highly evolved species whose environment is varied and variable; thus new ways of adjusting to it and new or more efficient methods of living in relation to it are constantly necessary, at times even vital. But new adaptations and new solutions cannot come about easily or be implanted firmly either through biological changes or by the utilisation of some of the mutations, or the process of learning in the less encumbered and more pliable young—unless death exists to make room for the new by carrying off the old. Gardeners know only too well how ruthlessly one must prune in order to give new vigour to the young shoots.

In the case of man we are confronted with another dimension—beyond the purely physical and biological facts. Man lives in society and is poorly endowed with ready-made instinctual patterns of reaction; but he is entrusted with consciousness and hence conscious knowledge of his own future death, and therefore with the question that burns in him continuously: 'What is it all about? What is the meaning of it all?' He is, moreover, also encumbered with self-consciousness, and with the capacity to observe the operations of his mind, his psyche, separately and independently of his actions. Here lies the root of the most essentially human function—symbolisation. And because symbols, as they evolve, not only affect the development and the behaviour of the individual but also influence the development and behaviour of whole groups, the cycle of the death of old symbols and the creation of new symbols is as imperative and has at least as much impact as the biological mutations. Thus, as on the physical level so also on the psychic one, there can be no birth without risk, confusion, disorientation and pain.

CHAPTER 5

Summary

To sum up: It is my principal thesis that those who would die well and those who would create well are people who must be capable of being open and available both to the life forces and the death forces; and so they are available on the one hand to the processes of differentiation and integration, and on the other, to the processes of de-differentiation. In other words, they are people who can think and test and learn and assume control and responsibility, but they can also let go of these faculties and bear doubt and chaos and not-knowing, without excessive panic or pain or resentment. In other words, they are people who can sacrifice their phantasies of omnipotence. Instead they can learn, acquire skills, concentrate and take account of both extra- and intra-psychic reality; and they can also make themselves available to feelings of awe and wonder, which are the acknowledgment and the experience of mystery.

Only through more discussion, however, a greater pooling of clinical data and further study of biographies, can we hope to discover whether, in fact, the person who can live and work creatively is also able to die creatively.

I feel that I cannot bring this book to a more appropriate ending or describe my thesis more convincingly than by quoting a poem. A single sheet, it fell out of a book I was reading, by sheer chance, while I prepared my own. The poet is unknown to me. But his poem expresses, at least for me, in a few powerful words and rhythms what all these chapters have laboured at.

> i pin my hopes on quiet
>
> slow processes
>
> tearing flaring near despairing
> clawing gnawing ever warring
> hither thither
> this way that and

round and round and
in and out
til chaos
    Chaos
      CHAOS

the tempest falters
frag
    ments
      fall and
fumbling
find a fuller form

you
speak
an island life of thought
is moved to action

you
smile
a tight gloved heart
stirs

dark funnel's
distant gleam
beckons

begun 1961: completed 1971.
John C Pritchard

Postscript

As I bring this book to a close I cannot prevent myself from expressing some profound apprehension at what we, the psychologists, may in fact be perpetrating, by probing those depths of man, where he faces his two most crucial moments: the moment of creation and the moment of death. By revealing and by making generally known some of the experiences that are going on inside him, can we be certain that we are not robbing him of his capacity for spontaneous and genuine surrender to the forces that act upon him while he is travailing in order to create or to die? Once this knowledge is really well disseminated, will people still be able to regress truly, neither hindering it nor forcing it? Will they really remain able to 'relate' to the unconscious and unknown inside them—or shall we have encouraged them to try to seduce it or even to rape it, in order that it may yield up its gifts of inspiration? Will people still be able to 'die their own death'? And will their death really be a true dying, a surrender and not, like suicide, a manipulation?

What comforts me a little when I pose these questions to myself is that, in spite of our great knowledge of the psychology of dreaming, we do still dream.

References

ABRAHAMSON, H. (1958). *The origin of death: Studies in African mythology.* Princeton University (unpublished).

ARIES, P. (1974). *Western attitudes toward death.* Baltimore, Johns Hopkins University Press.

ARNHEIN, R. (1966). *Towards a psychology of art.* London, Faber.

AUDEN, W. H. (1962). 'Making, knowing and judging', in *The dyer's hand.* London, Faber.

BALINT, M. (1968). *The basic fault.* London, Tavistock.

BEAUVOIR, S. (1946). *Tous les hommes sont mortels.* Paris, Gallimard.

BELLAK, L. (1952). *Manic-depressive psychoses and allied conditions.* New York, Grune & Stratton.

BERGSON, H. (1911). *Creative evolution.* New York, Mitchell.

BLAKE, W. (1969). *Complete writings.* Oxford University Press.

BOWLBY, J. (1961). 'The process of mourning'. *Int. J. Psycho-Anal.,* **42,** 4–5.

BROWN, N. (1959). *Life against death.* London, Routledge & Kegan Paul.

BRUN, R. (1953). 'On Freud's hypothesis of the death instinct'. *Psyche,* Heidelberg.

CASSIRER, E. (1953). *An essay on man.* New York, Doubleday.

CLARK, K. (1971). *An art historian's apology.* (Cosmos Club Award Lecture), Washington.

COLERIDGE, S. T. (1971). *Biographia literaria.* London, Dent, Everyman series.

DAVIDSON, D. (1966). 'Transference as a form of active imagination'. *J. analyt. Psychol.,* **11,** 2.

DEUTSCH, H. (1965). 'Absence of grief', in *Neuroses and character types.* New York, International Universities Press.

DUNNE, J. S. (1974). *The city of the gods.* London, Sheridan Press.

EHRENZWEIG, A. (1967). *The hidden order of art.* London, Weidenfeld & Nicolson.

EINSTEIN, A. (1956). *The world as I see it.* London, Souvenir Press.

EISSLER, K. R. (1955). *The psychiatrist and the dying patient.* New York, International Universities Press.

ELIADE, M. (1960). *Myths, dreams and mysteries.* London, Harvill Press.

FEDERN, P. (1953). *Ego psychology and the psychoses.* New York, Basic Books.

References

FEIFEL, H. (Ed.) (1955). *The meaning of death.* New York, McGraw-Hill.

FENICHEL, O. (1945). *The psycho-analytic theory of neurosis.* London, Routledge & Kegan Paul.

FIELD, D., NEWICK, J. (Eds.) (1973). *The study of education and art.* London, Routledge & Kegan Paul.

FLUEGEL, J. C. (1953). 'The death instinct'. *Int. J. Psycho-Anal.*, **34** (Supp.).

FORDHAM, M. (1957). *New developments in analytical psychology.* London, Routledge & Kegan Paul.

—— (1969). *Children as individuals.* London, Hodder & Stoughton.

FRAZER, J. (1950). *The golden bough.* London, Macmillan.

FREUD, A. (1957). Introduction to *On not being able to paint* by M. Milner. London, Heinemann.

FREUD, S. (1912). 'Recommendations for physicians, on the psychoanalytic method of treatment'. *Coll. papers*, **2**.

—— (1920). 'Beyond the pleasure principle'. *Coll. wks.*, **18**.

—— (1913). 'The theme of the three caskets'. *Coll. wks.*, **12**.

GORDON, R. (1963). 'Gods and the de-integrates'. *J. analyt. Psychol.*, **8**, 1.

—— (1965). 'The concept of projective identification'. *J. analyt. Psychol.*, **10**, 2.

—— (1972). 'A very private world', in *The function and nature of imagery* (ed. P. Sheehan). New York, Academic Press.

GORER, G. (1955). 'The pornography of death'. *Encounter*, **5**.

GREENACRE, P. (1971). 'The childhood of the artist', in *Emotional growth*, Vol. II. New York, International Universities Press.

HAUSER, A. (1951). *Social history of art.* London, Routledge & Kegan Paul.

—— (1959). *The philosophy of art.* London, Routledge & Kegan Paul.

HILLMAN, J. (1969). 'On psychological creativity'. *Art International*, XIII, **7**, p. 27.

HINTON, J. (1967). *Dying.* Harmondsworth, Penguin Books.

HOFFMAN, F. (1955). 'Mortality and modern literature', in *The meaning of death* (H. Feifel). New York, McGraw-Hill.

HOUSMAN, A. E. (1933). *The name and nature of poetry.* London, Macmillan.

JACOBSON, E. (1965). *The self and the object world.* London, Hogarth.

JENNINGS, E. (1961). *Every changing shape.* London, Deutsch.

JENNINGS, S. (1975). *Creative therapy.* London, Pitman.

JUNG, C. G. (1912). *Symbols of transformation. Coll. wks.*, **5**.

—— (1928). *Two essays on analytical psychology. Coll. wks.*, **7**.

—— (1928). 'On psychic energy', in *Coll. wks.*, **8**.

—— (1930). 'The stages of life'. *Coll. wks.*, **8**.

JUNG, C. G. (1931). 'The secret of the golden flower'. *Coll. wks.*, **13**.
—— (193 5). 'The transcendent function', in *Coll. wks.*, **8**.
—— (1935). 'Psychological commentary on *The Tibetan book of the dead'*. *Coll. wks.*, **11**.
KAHNWEILER, D. H. (1950). *Klee*. Paris. Les Editions Braun & Cie.
KASTENBAUM, R. (1955). 'Time and death and adolescence', in *The meaning of death* (H. Feifel). New York, McGraw-Hill.
KHAN, M. (1974). *The privacy of the self*. London, Hogarth.
KLEIN, M. (1952). 'Theory of anxiety and guilt', in *Developments in psycho-analysis*. London, Hogarth.
KOESTLER, A. (1964). *The act of creation*. London, Hutchinson.
KUBLER-ROSS, E. (1969). *On death and dying*. London, Macmillan.
LANDSBERG, P. L. (1953). *The experience of death*. London, Rockliffe.
LANGER, S. (1941). *Philosophy in a new key*. Oxford University Press.
McCULLY, R. (1963). 'Fantasy productions of children with a progressively crippling and fatal illness'. *J. Genetic Psychol.*, **102**, pp. 203–216.
MACKINNON, D. W. (1970). 'The personality correlates of creativity: a study of American architects', in *Creativity*, ed. P. E. Vernon. Harmondsworth, Penguin Books.
MADURO, R. (1977). 'Symbolic motives in creative process: a Jungian contribution', in *Art and culture: approaches to process and change* (ed. N. Graburn). University of New Mexico Press.
MILNER, M. (1939). *An experiment in leisure*. London, Chatto & Windus.
—— (1957). *On not being able to paint*. London, Heinemann.
NEUMANN, E. (1959). *Art and the creative unconscious*. London, Routledge & Kegan Paul.
NOON, J. A. (1944). 'A preliminary examination of the death concept of the Ibo'. *American Anthropologist*.
PHILIPSON, M. (1963). *Outline of a Jungian aesthetic*. Evanston, North-western University Press.
PLAUT, A. (1977). 'Jung and rebirth'. *J. analyt. Psychol.*, **22**, 2.
RANK, O. (1952). *The trauma of birth*. New York, Brunner.
READ, H. (1964). *The philosophy of modern art*. London, Faber.
—— (1965). *Icon and idea*. London, Faber.
—— (1967. *Art and alienation*. London, Thames & Hudson.
—— (1960). *The form of things unknown*. London, Faber.
REDFEARN, J. (1970). 'Bodily experience in psychotherapy'. *Brit. J. med. Psychol.*, **43**, 4.
REID, L. A., (1969). *Meaning in the arts*. London, Allen & Unwin.
RILKE, R. M. (1961). *The book of hours*. London, Thames & Hudson.
RUGG, H. (1963). *Imagination*. New York, Harper & Row.
SCHNEIDER, D. (1950). *The psycho-analyst and the artist*. New York, Mentor Books.

SEARLES, H. (1965). *Collected papers on schizophrenia and related subjects.* London, Hogarth.

SEGAL, H. (1955). 'A psycho-analytic approach to aesthetics', in *New directions in psycho-analysis.* London, Tavistock.

SHEEHAN, P. (1972). *The function and nature of imagery.* New York, Academic Press.

STEIN, L. (1957). 'What is a symbol supposed to be?'. *J. analyt. Psychol.,* **2**, 1.

SWIFT, J. (1726). *Gulliver's travels.* Oxford University Press.

TILLICH, P. (1955). 'The eternal now', in *The meaning of death* (ed. H. Feifel). New York, McGraw-Hill.

WILLIAMS, M. (1963). 'The indivisibility of the personal and collective unconscious'. *J. analyt. Psychol.,* **8**, 1.

—— (1966). 'Changing attitudes to death'. *Human relations.*

WINNICOTT, D. W. (1958). *Collected papers.* London, Tavistock.

—— (1971). *Playing and reality.* London, Tavistock.

Glossary

This glossary is intended to show how I have used and how I think about certain terms in this book.

Active Imagination

A technique evolved by Jung in order to facilitate a form of internalised analytic process: the conscious ego takes on the function of the observing and receptive analyst in the presence of freely flowing images, affects and phantasies.

Aggression

The fighting instinct in beast and man. It helps distribute members over the available habitat, selects the best fitted for reproduction, establishes hierarchical order and, in the individual, helps to establish boundaries and independence. It thus helps the survival of individual and species. But in man the aggressive impulse is often associated with the death urge—i.e. it can become mixed up with other basic drives—in the absence of sufficiently reliable ritualised aggression-inhibitions possessed by most other carnivores.

Archetypal Formal Patterns

Certain formal patterns which occur fairly universally and tend to provoke similar sensuous, emotional and symbolic reactions, e.g. the circle, the square, the spiral, the ellipse, the mandala, etc. Certain colour and sound patterns are also likely to have archetypal qualities.

Archetypal Images

The form through which archetypal processes can become visible, conscious and hence experienced. According to Jung archetypal images represent the goals of the instincts.

Archetypal Personages

Personages experienced either in phantasy or through projection onto an external person, characterised by the fact that they appear in different cultures, at different times and often feature in myths, fairy tales, art and literature; e.g. the great mother, the phallic mother, the eternal youth, the trickster, the witch, the magician, the wise old man, the divine child, etc.

Archetypal Themes

Themes that feature in the phantasy of individuals, and in myth, folklore and art in many cultures and in many different epochs, e.g. the hero's quest, the night-sea journey, virgin birth, the flood, etc.

Archetype

A metapsychological, a conceptual, model to account for the recurrence and apparent universality in man in different cultures and in different epochs of certain experiences and images, the archetypal images.

The activation of archetypal contents—whether personages, themes or sensuous patterns—is usually accompanied by strong affect and powerful phantasies.

Jung has described the archetype as a psychosomatic entity, whose physical expression takes the form of instinctive activity and its mental expression the form of images.

He has also compared them to the invisible presence of the crystal lattice in a saturated solution.

The archetypes, so Jung makes clear, are devoid of content to begin with until personal experience renders them visible and hence potentially conscious.

They may also be thought of as psychic 'programmers'.

The Area of Experience, or the Third Area

A concept developed by Winnicott.

The area of experience evolves out of an infant's attempt to reconcile reality and phantasy, inner world and outer world. The reconciliation of these two worlds is the foundation of this third area. This area then becomes the source of play, imagination, culture, religion and art, for it is here that man's capacity to symbolise develops.

The area of experience develops out of the infant's attachment to a transitional object (q.v.).

Jung's concept of 'psychic reality', we can now suggest, refers to the contents and the experience of this intermediate, this third area.

The Collective Unconscious

This is a concept developed by Jung. It refers to that part of the mind that contains impulses, drives and phantasies that have never yet been conscious but are characteristic of human beings in general. In other words, in the collective unconscious lies the communal and collective heritage of the species, man.

The degree of unconsciousness is likely to be greater in the collective unconscious than in the personal unconscious.

The Conscious

That area of experience which is available for knowledge and awareness.
'To be conscious' has really two connotations:

1. The state in which one is awake and aware; in other words, one is not asleep or anaesthetised or in a coma.
2. The state in which one is self-aware. This can be further sub-divided:

i. Primary self-awareness, which means that one knows and is aware of what one does and experiences;
ii. Reflective self-awareness. This means that one's own mental processes are the object of one's attention and reflection.

Creativity or the Creative Process

This involves making and/or discovering; it implies inventiveness, productivity and originality as well as the search for meaning, value and excellence.

It is heavily dependent on the capacity to symbolise and to play.

Dying and Creating: A Search for Meaning

Death Experience

I use this concept to refer to a psychological state in which one's individual boundaries seem to have ceased to exist and differentiation, separateness and the tension of opposites appear to have been eliminated.

Deintegrate

That which differentiates out of the matrix of the self through the process of deintegration.

Like the ethologist's 'innate release mechanism', the deintegrate potentiates a '*readiness* for experience, a readiness to perceive and act', even though 'there is as yet no perception or action' (Fordham).

The concept of the deintegrate is almost identical to that of the archetypal image, but the word itself reminds one of its provenance and that it is therefore a 'piece of the self'. These precipitates of the process of deintegration then become the bricks and mortar that help build up and consolidate the ego and its function; at the same time, because of their origins and their links with the self, they play an important rôle in the play of phantasy and imagination, and so mediate experiences of awe, wonder and awareness of the very existence of the non-ego within the psyche.

Deintegration

'The spontaneous division of the self into parts—a manifest necessity if consciousness is ever to arise ... It is the spontaneous property of the self behind ego formation' (Fordham).

Dying

I have used 'dying' to denote the experience, not of a state, like death, but of a process, a movement that is, or is experienced as, a change from the state of being alive to a state of being dead.

Ego

That part of the psyche which evolves out of the original self through maturational processes. Its primary goal and function is the making and the preserving of consciousness, and of the sense of personal identity and continuity. It also mediates between drives and affects on the one hand, and reality and its testing on the other.

Ego Identity

The sense of confidence that there is an inner continuity and meaningful cohesion which is experienced by oneself and recognised by others. It finds expression in the relative accuracy and sharpness of definition of the body-image and the ego-image.

Eros, or the Life Force

One of the two primary drives, the other being Thanatos, whose existence is postulated in order to account for man's need to live, to survive, to procreate and to experience fear when in danger.

The goal of Eros, or the life force, is de-fusion, separateness and identity; it is therefore particularly involved in the development and establishment of the ego.

Ethology

A term originally employed by J. S. Mill to designate the 'Science of Character'. In modern times Tinbergen, a follower of Konrad Lorenz, has used this term for the new science, the 'scientific study of animal behaviour'. This is essentially concerned with the experimental investigation of the bio-physiology of instinct.

Fusion Experience

This is a psychological experience—*not* a material fact.

It is the experience of such great closeness that the boundary between self and other seems to have melted away, and only a joint identity can be experienced.

Such experiences can at times exist between mother and foetus, between mother and new-born infant, between lovers in sexual intercourse and in religious and artistic ecstasy.

Illusion

Cf. 'transitional object'.

'. . . that which is allowed to the infant, and which in adult life is inherent in art and religion and yet becomes the hallmark of madness when an adult puts too powerful a claim on the credulity of others, forcing them to acknowledge a sharing of illusion that is not their own' (Winnicott).

Image

The perception of sensory data like forms, colours, sounds, smells, movements, objects, etc., in the absence of an actual external stimulus which could have caused such a perception. It is the representation of a sensuous and individual experience.

External stimuli may of course have been present in the past, and the image is practically always dependent on such past experiences.

Imagination

The coalescence of images into a dramatic form so that they tell a story which has not only cognitive content but above all emotional urgency and meaning. The image is like a still picture; imagination is like a moving film.

Identification

A process by which a person fuses or confuses his own identity with someone else's.

It is a process similar to that of introjection (q.v.); but it is in fact more sophisticated since it concerns whole clusters of personal identity and so depends on both the perception and the possession of more consolidated ego structures than is involved in introjection.

Individuation

A process that Jung has explored with particular care and interest and that he has regarded as of quite unique value in man's psychic development.

The process of individuation involves a readiness for ever greater awareness of one's own nature, with its positive as well as its negative tendencies and qualities, leading to an ever clearer understanding of who one is. Thus one's self-image becomes ever more appropriate and is accompanied by a growing recognition of one's separateness and one's personal responsibility; but all this happens in the context of an acceptance that there exist processes beyond our control and comprehension.

Thus individuation aims at the achievement of optimum synthesis of conscious and unconscious processes and phantasies. It leads a person to experience his own individual uniqueness together with the recognition that there are forces both within and without him that transcend his personal and conscious understanding.

In consequence the process of individuation encompasses the process of individualisation, though it moves a person beyond this essentially ego-building process towards the search for values, meaning and self-transcendence.

Innate Fixed Pattern

A concept evolved by the new science, ethology.

A hierarchical organised nervous mechanism which is susceptible to certain primary releasing and directing impulses of internal as well as of external origin, and which responds to these impulses by co-ordinated movements that contribute to the maintenance of the individual and the species.

Innate Release Mechanism (I.R.M.)

A concept evolved by the new science, ethology.

A special neuro-sensory mechanism that releases a reaction and is responsible for its selective susceptibility to a particular special combination of sign-stimuli. The existence of I.R.M. is suggested by the strict dependence of a reaction upon a specific set of sign-stimuli.

Instinct

That correlate of structural physiological, behavioural and experiential features, established by heredity, which is activated in a co-ordinated manner when the organism encounters the relevant or matching situation in its environment. It is then composed of a congenital impulse plus specific emotional excitement.

Introjection

The process by which the qualities or functions of an object or a person external to the individual are incorporated, absorbed and so put inside him and then experienced as an inner, personal possession.

Libido

Jung uses the concept 'libido' as synonymous with 'psychic energy', irrespective of the particular area or channel into which it happens to have been drawn.

This contrasts with Freud's use of the term libido. In his first formulation he thought of libido as the energy attached specifically to the sexual instincts; in his second formulation he distinguished ego-libido from object-libido; and in his third formulation he defined libido as the energy of Eros or the life instinct, while another form of energy was thought to be attached to Thanatos, the death instinct (q.v.), an energy that has so far remained nameless although some have attempted to coin the names 'mortido' or 'destrudo'. These names have not caught on.

Original Self

The original state of wholeness that characterises the psychic life of the baby in the first few days of life. It is the early form of what later becomes a complex state and a sophisticated goal. Such a concept implies that development proceeds from simple order to ever-increasing complex order.

The predominance of this psychic institution favours the experience of fusion; the later developing institution of the self favours the experience of unification.

Participation Mystique

A term Jung had found in the writings of the anthropologist, Lévy-Bruhl. It denotes the peculiar kind of psychological connection between a subject and an object in which the identity of the two are fused and confused.
Cf. projective identification.

Personal Unconscious

That part of the psyche which contains those mental processes—impulses, wishes, fears, memories—of which the subject is not aware. They have been relegated there by the process of repression because they are suspected of creating pain, discomfort or moral repugnance.

Playing

'The manipulation of external phenomena in the service of the dream' (Winnicott).

Play is distinguished from all other activities because its *primary* goal is to foster personal growth. It is therefore above all in the service of individuation.

Play is based on, and is an expression of, the process of symbolisation, and is continuous with the creative process and with cultural experience.

Poemagogic Images

A term coined by Ehrenzweig in order to describe those images that express 'those self-destructive processes which are in fact inherent in all *creative* work'. These images have then the special function of both inducing and of symbolising the ego's creativity. As an example he cites the ubiquitous myth of the white goddess and her dead son-lover which was quoted by Marion Milner in her book, *An experiment in leisure.*

Projection

Attributing to something—or more usually to someone—in one's environment a personal characteristic, feeling or impulse that is experienced as 'bad' and therefore as pain-making or shame-making. Occasionally some 'good' part of oneself may undergo such projection, either in order to protect this 'good' part from destruction or contamination by the 'bad' parts inside oneself, or else as a means of reassuring oneself that the external world is safe and good.

When the content projected is felt to be a part of one's own self one might speak of 'ex-nuclear projection', while projection of an inner figure—an internalised parent, sibling, etc.—might be named 'ex-orbital projection'. The names for this distinction have been taken from John Wisdom (1961), who used these terms in order to differentiate two forms of introjection.

Projection can be viewed as the psychic equivalent of excretion.

Projective Identification

A concept developed by Klein. It is a process which Jung seems to refer to when he speaks of 'participation mystique', 'primitive identity', or 'psychic infection'. It

177

is a psychological mechanism which aims to re-establish the experience of fusion; it involves the mixing and muddling up of subject and object, inner world and outer world and hence the undoing of boundaries.

Psychic Energy

A hypothetical life energy resulting from the tension of the opposing life and death forces.

Psychic Reality

The experience we have, whether or not it has been produced by a material fact or a tangible cause. Consequently a functional stomach-ache is a psychic reality, that is a reality in and for the psyche, even if there is no somatic reason to account for it. And a hallucination of a mouse under the table is a psychic reality, whether or not there is an actual mouse or a mouse-like object present.

Psychic reality is thus the stuff that belongs to what Winnicott has now termed the 'area of experience'.

Reductive Analysis

That part of analysis which concerns itself with tracing back complex and differentiated behaviour and experience to earlier and simpler events and psychological structures. It is concerned with causes and the reconstruction of a person's history.

It is contrasted with what Jung has called the constructive or synthetic method.

Self

A metapsychological construct that serves, in an experiential model, to account for the experience of symbols of completion and totality: it is then also the source of those drives that seek and strive for wholeness, and here experiences of fusion, union and hence omnipotence prevail.

But in a structural model the self refers to the wholeness of the psyche and then includes the conscious as well as the unconscious areas of the psyche.

Symbol

Etymologically, 'throwing together such things as have something in common' (Stein).

'Symbol brings the idea and the image into an indivisible unity, so that the transformation of the image also implies the metamorphosis of the idea. The symbol can only be interpreted, it cannot be solved' (Hauser).

A symbol is like a bridge that links strange to familiar, conscious to unconscious, here-and-now to general and abstract, soma to psyche, fragment to whole and reason to passion. In a symbol, form is intimately relevant to content.

Symbolic Attitude

The 'as-if' attitude which ensures that that which does the signifying is not confused with that which is signified.

Symbolic Equation

The symbol and the object symbolised are felt and treated as though they were identical; in other words, the existence and characteristics of one of them is denied or not yet recognised, because it has been totally assimilated in the other.

The Symbolic Function

Also named the 'transcendent function' by Jung. It refers to that process which links the conscious to the unconscious and the strange to the familiar; its form is intimately relevant to its content. It is characterised by the 'as-if' attitude and so facilitates the experience of representation, not identification; consequently it involves the recognition of similarities in objects that are, at the same time, known to be separate and distinct. This then enables men to relate to unobservable realities in terms of observable phenomena and so mediate the experience of the world as having meaning and significance.

The Synthetic Method of Analysis

That part of analysis which Jung has contrasted to the reductive method. Here the unconscious products are examined in terms of their anticipatory function, and as expression that represents a potential psychological development in the future. In Jung's own words, the interpretative approach aims to discover a meaning from the unconscious product which is definitely related to the subject's future attitude.

Thanatos, or the Death Force

One of the two primary drives—the other being Eros—whose existence is postulated in order to account for the fact that man can live without going mad even though he knows that he is mortal and that, inevitably, one day he will die; the fact that most people succeed in going to their death in a more or less prepared and dignified manner, and that in fact throughout history men and women have often been ready to expose themselves to death for the sake of the future, their children, a belief, etc.

Thanatos or the death force is expressed in man's longing for fusion and non-differentiation, and I regard it as the valence and the attracting force of the self.

Transcendent Function

Cf. 'The symbolic function'.

Transference

Transference is that relationship in which the perception and the experience one person has of another is determined primarily, not by the reality and the characteristics of that other person, but by the inner situation of the percipient—by his experiences, expectations, complexes, phantasies, feelings, etc.

Transference is the result of the projection of unintegrated parts; since projection is an unconscious process these parts are on the whole unconscious, repressed or split off from consciousness. 'The transference phenomena is an inevitable feature of every thorough analysis, for it is imperative that the doctor should get into the closest possible touch with the patient's line of psychological development' (Jung).

Transitional Object

This is the object to which an infant or a very young child shows a particularly strong attachment and to which he clings for comfort. This transitional object is both given—it is in fact an object that exists in outer reality—but it is also created; for the infant imbues it with meaning and qualities which derive from his inner world.

179

According to Winnicott the transitional object represents *not* the fusion but the union of the infant and its mother, both of whom he is beginning to experience as separate beings.

The experience of the transitional object lays the foundation for the development of the area of experience, the third area.

'Transitional objects and transitional phenomena belong to the realm of illusion, which is at the basis of the initiation of experience . . . Its development is favoured or hindered according to whether the mother can allow the infant the illusion that what he creates really exists . . . and that she will not ask: Did you conceive of this or was it presented to you from without?' (Winnicott).

Index

Index

Index

Index